T0349019

Mastering VMware Cloud Disaster Recovery and Ransomware Resilience

A Practical Guide on VMware Cloud Disaster and Ransomware Recovery SaaS Solution

Christophe Lombard

Apress®

Mastering VMware Cloud Disaster Recovery and Ransomware Resilience:
A Practical Guide on VMware Cloud Disaster and Ransomware Recovery
SaaS Solution

Christophe Lombard
Triel sur seine, France

ISBN-13 (pbk): 979-8-8688-0828-9   ISBN-13 (electronic): 979-8-8688-0829-6
https://doi.org/10.1007/979-8-8688-0829-6

Managing Director, Apress Media LLC: Welmoed Spahr
Acquisitions Editor: Aditee Mirashi
Desk Editor: James Markham
Editorial Project Manager: Kripa Joseph
Copy Editor: Mary Behr

Cover designed by eStudioCalamar

Cover image designed by Marie-Amélie Lombard

Distributed to the book trade worldwide by Springer Science+Business Media New York, 1 New York Plaza, Suite 4600, New York, NY 10004-1562, USA. Phone 1-800-SPRINGER, fax (201) 348-4505, e-mail orders-ny@springer-sbm.com, or visit www.springeronline.com. Apress Media, LLC is a California LLC and the sole member (owner) is Springer Science + Business Media Finance Inc (SSBM Finance Inc). SSBM Finance Inc is a **Delaware** corporation.

For information on translations, please e-mail booktranslations@springernature.com; for reprint, paperback, or audio rights, please e-mail bookpermissions@springernature.com.

Apress titles may be purchased in bulk for academic, corporate, or promotional use. eBook versions and licenses are also available for most titles. For more information, reference our Print and eBook Bulk Sales web page at www.apress.com/bulk-sales.

Any source code or other supplementary material referenced by the author in this book is available to readers on GitHub. For more detailed information, please visit https://www.apress.com/gp/services/source-code.

If disposing of this product, please recycle the paper

To my wife and daughter.

To my readers who decided to pick this book!

Table of Contents

About the Author

Christophe Lombard is an IT architect with 26 years of experience in designing and delivering complex solutions in both consultative and technical leadership with a specific focus on cloud and IT transformation. He has worked within large organizations like NEC, CSC, EMC, and DELL, and more recently in a startup called Cloudreach. He has helped dozens of IT professionals and organizations achieve their business objectives through business and consultative engagements. During his career, he has served as a network engineer, project manager, consultant, and cloud architect.

He started developing his knowledge in VMware in 2005 and his cloud expertise in 2015. He is passionate about the development of innovation in companies using new technologies: cloud, IaaS, infrastructure as code, microservices, and big data. His two areas of expertise opened a door for him at VMware in 2020 during the pandemic.

As a lead cloud solution architect, Christophe helps drive VMware Cloud on AWS and VMware Cloud Disaster Recovery products adoption with key customers. He loves to learn, to enable, and to educate people including customers, partners, and colleagues on all the cloud technologies he is focused on.

Christophe holds an AWS Certified Solution Architect - Associate certification and has the following VMware certifications: VMware Cloud (VCP-VMC) 2022, VCP & VCAP DCV, VCP & VCAP - Design NV 2021, and vExpert 2021/2022/2023. Christophe also promotes and shares his knowledge on VMware technology and cloud solutions on his blog at vminded.com.

In his spare time, he enjoys working on his creative pursuits such as photography. Find Christophe at linkedin.com/in/lombardchristophe.

About the Technical Reviewer

 **Iwan Hoogendoorn** started his IT career in 1999 as a helpdesk agent. Soon after, Iwan started to learn Microsoft products and this resulted in his MCP, MCSA, MCDBA, and MCSE certifications. While working as a Microsoft systems engineer, Iwan gained an excellent basis to develop additional skills and knowledge in computer networking. Networking became a passion in his life. This passion resulted in learning networking with Cisco products.

He got the opportunity to work for VMware in 2016 as a senior NSX PSO consultant. In his time at VMware, he gained more knowledge on private and public clouds and the related products that VMware developed to build the Software Define Data Center (SDDC). Because new technology grows at a fast pace (especially within VMware and the VMware cloud space), Iwan plays catch-up all the time and tries to keep up with the new VMware presents. After working for four years as a senior NSX PSO consultant (primarily with VMware NSX-v and NSX-T), Iwan got promoted to a staff SDDC consultant focusing on the full SDDC stack including hyperscaler offerings on main public clouds like AWS (VMC on AWS), Microsoft (Azure VMware Solution), and Google (Google Cloud VMware Engine).

Iwan is certified on multiple VMware products, including NSX, and he is actively working with VMware certification to develop network-related exams for VMware. Iwan is also AWS and TOGAF certified.

Acknowledgments

I would like to thank my manager (and my friend!) at VMware, Luca Zerminiani, who has been helpful and supportive during my time at VMware as a solution architect. I would also like to thank my teammates Charlotte and Sébastien; you were the best! Thank you to James Ellis for teaching me anything around the VMware Cloud Disaster Recovery solution.

To finish, thank you to the VMware family, my best company ever and good luck to the ones who are continuing the story under the Broadcom umbrella.

Introduction

Thank you for picking up *Mastering VMware Cloud Disaster Recovery and Ransomware Resilience.* This is my second book with Apress and I hope you will find it valuable.

I wrote this book because I think ransomware is one of the most important matters for IT managers today. But I also want to focus attention on ransomware recovery, a topic that is often underestimated and wrongly covered by IT organizations.

This book is divided into three chapters covering the topic of ransomware recovery and the VMware approach to solving the challenges of ransomware through the Live Cyber Recovery solution.

The first chapter covers the business context of ransomware recovery. You will learn the importance of DR in the modern IT landscape, the challenge of the growing threat of ransomware, and how to implement an optimal disaster recovery strategy. I finish the chapter by introducing the VMware Live Cyber Recovery solution, including the high-level architecture of the solution, its value proposition, and the most common use cases it addresses.

If you are someone who's been tasked with implementing or administering a ransomware recovery solution, Chapter 2 is for you. In it you will learn how the VMware Live Cyber Recovery solution can help implement a true DR-as-a-service approach to disaster or ransomware recovery. You will learn how to implement the solution, how to interconnect it, how to set up a DR environment, and how to implement a DR strategy. I finish the chapter by covering the operational aspects of the solution.

If you are more interested in ransomware, in Chapter 3 I cover ransomware threat and recovery strategies. I address ransomware, the type of ransomware attacks, and the challenge of recovering after a ransomware attack. In the final part of the chapter, I show you how the VMware Live Cyber recovery workflow can help you address the challenge of recovering your precious data after a ransomware attack.

The best alternative to recovering after a disaster such as ransomware is a solid recovery plan with a well-established process and a solution with critical key capabilities.

If you are interested to know more about this, please follow me in this book and learn how to implement the best ransomware recovery approach.

Preface

We are living in an ever-changing world where uncertainty, increased exposure to external threats or malicious actors, and diverse security risks are the common denominators of our life. The level of threat is getting higher and higher in this context where new geopolitical tensions are exacerbated and clearly contribute additional fears.

If we look at current cybersecurity threats and try to identify the attackers and their motives, we see that it's not only limited to hackers or script kiddies trying to have fun and get popularity, but also cybercriminals and state-sponsored groups that target critical infrastructure to steal data and extort financial gains (a recent Palo Alto study affirms that financially motivated ransomware attacks are up 37% this year compared to 2022).

Cyber attackers use a variety of techniques to compromise systems, steal data, or disrupt operations—from phishing and social engineering to denial of service, malware, and ransomware—and the landscape of cyber threats is continually evolving. The rise of generative artificial intelligence marks a new level of risk for cybersecurity as it adds a new level in the sophistication of attacks. It also means hackers can be more productive, efficient, and strike faster and more frequently than ever.

To achieve this, attackers continue to perfect the techniques that allow them to penetrate information systems, propagate and exfiltrate information, or position themselves to avoid being detected.

We can say that we are living in a never-before-seen unsecured world.

PREFACE

As the level of threat keeps growing, for IT managers it means an increased amount of resources, time, and money needs to be mobilized. Strategic and industrial spies push them to protect sensitive data at a higher level with more sophisticated solutions and set up both preventive and recovery measures with ransomware recovery features.

Traditional solutions may represent risks because they present technical weaknesses and offer less flexible operating models with manual and error-prone processes. Organizations need to invest in a modern ransomware recovery approach based on a dedicated workflow and an air-gapped immutable storage component as that's the only way to reach their objectives of zero trust and trusted availability for their critical assets.

CHAPTER 1

Introduction: Disaster Recovery Business Context

1.1 Importance of Disaster Recovery in the Modern IT Landscape

Although it would be utopian to try to foresee and master and control everything, the head of an organization—whether public or private—must design and implement protection strategies to avoid certain events, or at least to limit their direct impact on the organization's objectives and to ensure business continuity despite the loss of critical resources.

The nature, frequency, and cost of crises have changed significantly over the past 20 years. There is no doubt how closely intertwined are the various dimensions of these events, which have a major impact on disrupting the operations of many public and private organizations, with consequences that can go as far as definitive shutdown of activity.

Disaster recovery (DR) has always been a challenge in the history of IT. Overall, an IT organization can be exposed to diverse risks including power outages, site destruction, pandemic, fire, flood, vulnerabilities exploitation, tornados, and more.

© Christophe Lombard 2024
C. Lombard, *Mastering VMware Cloud Disaster Recovery and Ransomware Resilience*, https://doi.org/10.1007/979-8-8688-0829-6_1

From a risk perspective, most of the time the IT managers are considering things as an "if" type of event and not a "when." It could happen but it will probably not. This can mean that the investment in and frequency of testing of their DR plan are quite insufficient.

With the rise of ransomware, most businesses and cyber insurance companies consider it as a disaster that's likely going to happen regardless of the good security measures in place.

This is why it's very important to develop a DR strategy. It all starts by evaluating the level of risks, understanding the consequences of the occurrence of a disaster scenario, and making sure you have the right process and tooling to limit the consequences.

Starting a risk analysis process implies defining all risks and understanding how each identified risk can affect the company's operations. The plan should also include what safeguards and procedures should be implemented to mitigate the risks and testing the mitigation procedures to ensure they work.

Risk analysis is a process often carried out by the IT security manager and is based on three elements:

- A management approach

- A risk model

- Metrics to quantify the risk level

Once the risk analysis has been done, it's time to make sure there is a well-managed Business Continuity Plan (BCP) in place. This means having a clear process that considers the security requirements to develop and maintain business continuity throughout the organization.

1.1.1 Best Practices to Implement a Business Continuity Plan

The business continuity strategy must be clearly described in a document called a Business Continuity Plan. The BCP represents the set of measures designed under various crisis scenarios, including even in the face of extreme shocks, to maintain the company's operations, in a degraded mode, if necessary, on a temporary basis, service delivery or other essential or important operational tasks, followed by a planned recovery of activities.

The BCP exists to help the organization continue operating in the event of threats or disruptions by providing the relevant guidance and implementing the right procedures to mitigate the risks. The BCP should include the following:

- **The context:** Business objectives and legal obligations of the company with a list of essential activities to reach the objectives (and a list of key processes)

- **A list of the most important risks** explicitly described through scenarios or by defining a complete analysis

- **The business continuity strategy** that describes the level of services needed and the maximum supported downtime for each essential activity

It should also include the following information:

- An inventory of all critical assets

- The results of a Business Impact Analysis (BIA)

- The frequency of the DR tests

It is mandatory that the BCP must be regularly reviewed to make sure it's still up to date and that it aligns with the priority of the organization as well as with any compliance and regulatory requirements and changes in the objectives and in the level of risk.

From the organizational perspective, the responsibility of creating, managing, and implementing the BCP requires a specific transverse team that includes all important stakeholders like the IT manager, business stakeholders, the CISO, and infrastructure team members. Every person in charge of an action in the BCP should precisely know their role.

Objectives of continuity for the applications need to be defined and well understood by every party from the business to IT stakeholders. Some important metrics that can be used to define those objectives are shown in Figure 1-1 and described here:

- **RPO** (Recovery Point Objective) represents the maximum amount of data that can be lost.

- **RTO** (Recovery Time Objective) is the maximum acceptable interruption time. It is the time before you can accept a downtime. Exceeding the maximum interruption period, which may result from the non-delivery of a product or service, would have unfavorable consequences that would be unacceptable for the organization's objectives or obligations.

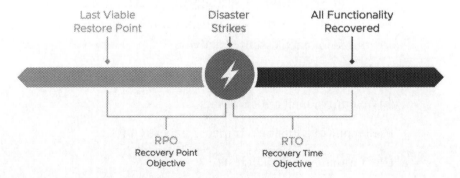

Figure 1-1. Business continuity metrics

Part of the BCP includes a Recovery Plan where steps to recover critical business functions are described in detail by the business. The Recovery Plan is crucial as it gives the required means to achieve the RPO and RTO and make sure the overall business continuity fulfills the business requirements.

It's important to distinguish a Business Continuity Plan from a Disaster Recovery Plan that focuses on technology and information technology.

The crisis management disposal enables the implementation of the BCP by steering response actions and uncertainty management through incident detection, qualification, escalation, alerts, mobilization, crisis cell activation, anticipation, intervention, triggering of BCP recommendations (palliative solution, recovery plan), and communication.

1.1.2 Examining the Challenges of DR Solutions

This is the role of the IT managers to delegate the design and deployment of the appropriate solutions to help address the business continuity strategy and implement the best DR plan to the infrastructure manager.

IT infrastructure managers should use a budget aligned on the business continuity objectives that address the business requirements and the criticality of each application. The more critical the application, the more it could potentially cost money when a disaster that generates an application downtime can occur.

Most customers consider whether they have implemented the right solutions to cover their business needs for DR and most of the time they rely on a traditional backup solution or an asynchronous data replication mechanism to a physical DR site.

This kind of DR solution presents some drawbacks, from operational complexity to higher cost and low reliability. Let's present the most relevant limitations of running such solutions:

- **OpEx-intensive:** Traditional DR solutions require a large initial investment in hardware and software because they necessitate building and maintaining a secondary site and installing, integrating, and supporting a mix of different solutions.

- **Inefficiency:** The DR site is sized for the worst case and there is often inefficient storage of copies. This also implies having to run and maintain resources that aren't necessary.

- **Complex infrastructure-centric setup:** The traditional DR approach requires you to integrate and maintain several solutions including a backup solution, storage, a replication mechanism, and some kind of automation and orchestration, which can be a complex task to address.

- **No lifecycle management:** The patchwork of siloed solutions implies no simple update, thus a need for manual operations or complicated upgrades.

- **Disruptive testing and unpredictable recovery times:** Orchestrating a DR test in production is complex because it is disruptive and error-prone, and it limits the ability or willingness to execute tests frequently. The direct consequence is that it makes the DR *unreliable.*

SaaS-based services abstract the complexity from DR operational and maintenance tasks.

1.2 The Growing Threat of Ransomware

Based on a survey conducted by Datrium—and echoed by many industry analyst surveys and other data sources—ransomware is the number one cause of DR events borne by businesses. For a complete view on the results please have a look at the Figure 1-2.

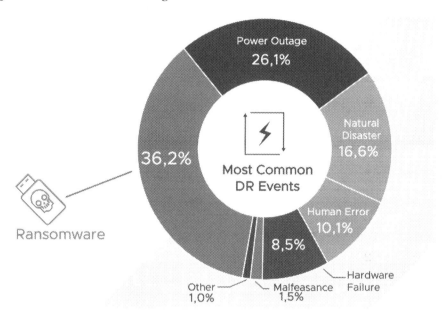

Figure 1-2. *State of enterprise resiliency and disaster recovery*

The other data point to consider here is the impact of these DR events. I have seen data that shows that the cost of downtime can be significant. In fact, IT downtime can cost upwards of $100K per day. And for about a quarter of organizations, this can go into the millions of dollars per day.

So, being able to recover from these sorts of events quickly before the impact to the business becomes irreversible is crucially important.

We are currently witnessing a paradigm shift in ransomware attacks. The landscape has changed substantially over the last five years. Scanning filesystems and recovery backup is not efficient enough because of the complexity of the attacks. The traditional approach is not working

7

anymore, and the complexity of the threat requires us to implement additional measures like an endpoint detection and response system (EDR), an isolated recovery environment (IRE), and to put in place a specific workflow.

In its latest annual Global Incident Response Threat[1] survey, VMware cybersecurity strategists found that the Zero Day exploit has shown no signs of abatement after a record level last year, and 62% of respondents said they have experienced ransomware in the past 12 months. In addition, there are several other threat areas, including new risks caused by deep fakes and container and cloud vulnerabilities.

The cost of ransomware has also increased due to the growing number of attacks coming from small, opportunistic ransomware groups, utilizing new and low-cost ransomware-as-a-service (RaaS) solutions, which have pushed the barrier to entry extremely low. The average ransom payment in Q2 2020 was $178,254. The latest Sophos State of Ransomware report of 2023 found the average ransom payment to be $1.54 million. This is almost double the 2022 figure and 10 times the 2020 figure!

The societal impact of ransomware is huge. Ransomware is today (and will continue to be) a top CIO budget priority.

Ransomware is a form of disaster that requires additional measures that need to be more sophisticated than the traditional recovery measures. Let's have a look at them.

---

[1] www.vmware.com/content/dam/learn/en/amer/fy23/pdf/1553238_Global_ Incident_Response_Threat_Report_Weathering_The_Storm.pdf

1.2.1 Ransomware Recovery Is a Critical Last Line of Defense

With the rise of ransomware, every customer will eventually require cyber recovery.

Let's have a look at the NIST framework for protection and ransomware recovery: identify, protect, detect, respond, and recover. These are the NIST-defined standard of the different phases on which sites should protect themselves with layers of protection. You can see an illustration of the steps or functions associated to the NIST framework on Figure 1-3.

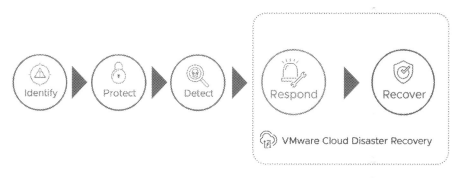

Figure 1-3. *NIST's five cybersecurity framework functions*

According to the NIST[2], a robust ransomware protection plan must have both preventative and recovery measures.

Preventative measures are security tools that can help prevent malware, threats, and ransomware from getting into the environment in the first place, and if it does, to contain and eradicate it before it causes widespread damage. This can be, for example, network and application firewalls,

---

[2] NIST is the National Institute of Standards and Technology at the U.S. Department of Commerce. The NIST Cybersecurity Framework helps businesses of all sizes better understand, manage, and reduce their cybersecurity risk and protect their networks and data.

intrusion detection systems, tooling for protection, and detection of attacks like intrusion or malware prevention systems. Most of the companies have an InfoSec team that takes care of implementing these solutions.

But now let's imagine a company is beaten by a Zero Day attack like what happened with Log4j or the SolarWinds supply chain attack, in which an organized cybercrime group exploited a Zero Day vulnerability to breach US government agencies and most of the Fortune 500. What can we do if all the preventive measures have been inefficient to protect the infrastructure and the data? What solutions do the IT managers and business have if all safeguards have failed?

Recovery measures are always required because preventative measures cannot make an organization fully immune to ransomware, and that is what I'm addressing here: the last two stages of ransomware recovery that serve as that critical last line of defense in case all preventative measures fail.

1.2.2 Challenges in Ransomware Recovery

Ransomware attacks are a very unpredictable form of malware. When you think about ransomware attacks, they come in different forms and sizes, and this makes it very difficult to plan the recovery effort without the proper tooling in place. Most of the time, traditional backup and disaster recovery solutions (which are focusing on restoring VMs) are not capable of providing a true ransomware recovery platform because they lack an isolated recovery environment and a way to quickly iterate the scanning of snapshots with Next Generation Antivirus (NGAV) or behavioral analysis.

Malicious codes use different tactics and techniques to infect your system and establish persistently, move laterally, and encrypt your workload. It's hard to know how you are going to be attacked.

It's difficult to anticipate the scale of the attack. It may be a few virtual machines or a large chunk of the VM estate that gets attacked.

Another unknown is the dwell time: how long the bad actors are on your system before you notice they are there. In smaller companies that don't have a large security team or budget, it can be up to 43 days. As the budget increases, and the security team presence increases, tooling gets better and the average dwell time is around 14 to 17 days on larger enterprise systems.

Let's discuss the top challenges in recovering from ransomware.

- **Identifying recovery point candidates**: This is the first stopping place when you think about what an infrastructure administrator is going to face. With appropriate retention schedules (six months is recommended for ransomware protection), there are going to be a lot of snapshots to look at. Identifying a good starting place is hard. Administrators may not know exactly when they were encrypted or originally infected. If they have a lot of workload to recover, it's a daunting task.

- **Validating the restore point**: How do you know it's a good one? Maybe it's not encrypted but what if the bad actors are still on the machine or if a restore point still has the malicious code?

- **Finally, limiting data loss**: When the system gets attacked, there is a good chance that you have already lost a few days of data, but it gets worse and worse the less prepared you are. When you have fewer options as far as restoration, data loss becomes a big problem.

1.3 Overview of VMware Live Cyber Recovery

VMware Live Cyber Recovery is a VMware-delivered, on-demand disaster-recovery-as-a-service (DRaaS) solution that can protect any on-premises vSphere environment with any vSphere storage, VMware Cloud on AWS (VMC), and Google Cloud VMware Engine (GCVE) from both disaster and ransomware attacks. It can achieve this by replicating the data out to a cloud disaster recovery service made of a SaaS-managed service and a proprietary technology developed by Datrium called the Scale-out Cloud File System (SCFS) that can store hundreds of recovery points with recovery point objectives (RPO[3]s) as low as 15 minutes.

It provides customers with a managed disaster and ransomware recovery solution with non-disruptive testing capabilities without the need to deploy a complex and costly secondary site.

As of March 2024, what was named VCDR or VCDR with Ransomware Recovery has been rebranded as VMware Live Cyber Recovery (VLCR) as part of the overall data protection branding strategy of VMware by Broadcom under VMware Live Recovery (VLR) next to and with the replacement of on-premises SRM, which is now named VMware Live Site Recovery (VLSR).

This book focuses exclusively on VMware Live Cyber Recovery.

1.3.1 High-Level Architecture

VMware Live Cyber Recovery Solution is a SaaS-based service that leverages cloud (VMware cloud-based managed services) as well as VMware Cloud on AWS as a recovery DR site. A description of the overall architecture is available on the Figure 1-4.

---

[3] Maximum age of files recovered from backup storage for normal operations to resume if a system goes offline as a result of a hardware, program, or communications failure.

It provides a very rapid ability to power on and get the workloads running on a VMware Cloud on AWS SDDC with a Pilot Light option for even faster RTO.

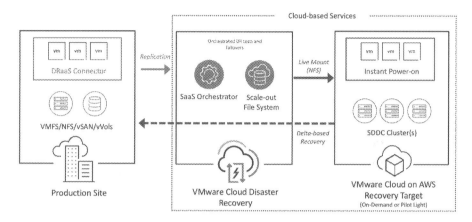

Figure 1-4. *VMware Live Cyber Recovery architecture*

The architecture of VMware Live Cyber Recovery consists of three main components:

- **Cyber Recovery Connector**: The Cyber Recovery Connector is a downloadable, lightweight virtual appliance that enables the protection of any vSphere workloads by creating snapshots of the virtual machine and replicating them securely to the cloud.

- **SaaS Orchestrator**: The SaaS Orchestrator serves as the UI where you can configure the settings and all relevant components needed to implement the DR strategy. This is where you define the frequency of your snapshots, the retention policy, and how the DR plans should be specified and executed. The role of the SaaS orchestrator is also to maintain compliance in your DR plan and make sure you can execute a failover when needed.

13

- **Scale-out cloud file system**: This is an air-gapped file system that allows for the VM replication to be stored securely and very efficiently. Every snapshot in the cloud file system is immutable. Data is never overwritten and can't be accessed, browsed, or changed. The second function of the SCFS is to create an NFS mount that can be presented to the recovery SDDC almost instantly. This is the minimum component that must be deployable to start protecting your workloads.

- **Recovery target**: Leveraging VMware Cloud on AWS, the recovery SDDC is where you run the recovered environment or applications. It is a cloud infrastructure that can scale automatically as workloads are restarted in case of a failover event. It is available in two modes: Pilot Light (for the lowest RTO) or on-demand, which removes the cost of running the recovery datacenter.

1.3.2 Value Proposition

VMware Live Cyber Recovery offers an on-demand ransomware and DRaaS with advanced isolated testing and restoration at scale. Gartner revealed in a study that isolated environments and immutable data vaults provide the highest level of security and recovery against insider threats, ransomware, and other forms of hacking. VMware Live Cyber Recovery is a great ransomware recovery platform with many capabilities as best practice to implement ransomware recovery, as stated by analysts like Gartner.

It offers the following:

- A deep snapshot history, from hours, days, or even up to months and they can be recovered without any RTO penalty.

- The system is operationally air-gapped.[4]

- Snapshots are immutable, which helps preserve the integrity of data.

- Instant power-on, which is important in regard to the pain point of selecting the right snapshot after a ransomware. Often the first selection is not the right one; it's an iterative process to find the right candidate, so instant power-on offers great time savings for that purpose.

- **File/folder level restore**: In the event you want to restore a VM before the bad guys even enter the system that may take you back three to four weeks and then pull files and folders from unencrypted workloads and put them in this cleaner snapshot.

- **An isolated recovery environment with VMware Cloud on AWS**: The IRE is a VMC SDDC preconfigured with a backup datastore. You can restore backups instantly into an SDDC (no data copy). VMC Cloud on AWS SDDC works very well as an isolated recovery environment. It's a "safe" place to spin up Ransomware Recovery (RWR) VMs to prevent your production environment from seeing reinfection; it's a sandbox environment. There are also custom network isolation levels in the IRE based on the NSX-T Advanced Firewall feature.

---

[4] An air gap is a security measure that involves isolating a computer or network and preventing it from establishing an external connection.

- **A dedicated ransomware recovery workflow**: If you look at the set of capabilities that support RWR, they are great. But imagine that as an admin you are going through processing an attack and recovering from it. Going into the process of creating your own workflow or runbook can be an error-prone task in the middle of an already stressful situation. What the solution offers is a dedicated workflow that guides users through the recovery process. This is an important feature from a time-savings perspective.

- **Guided restore point selection**: This means whenever you have that sea of snapshots to select from where to begin, the solution offers guidance on which snapshots are potentially encrypted. Thanks to this feature, you don't select those snapshots.

- **Pre-configured VM isolation levels**: This feature offers huge time savings to virtual infrastructure administrators when thinking about restoring multiple VMs and needing to bring them into isolation (they must go to NSX and configure it per the VM manually). You get push-button preconfigured isolation levels to remove the extra effort.

- **Behavioral analysis of powered-on VMs**: This is another great differentiator. Look at competitive offerings and see the way scanning is managed. Bad actors know that scanning for a file signature is easily avoided, and they do avoid it. Whenever bad actors go after systems, they tend to use "file less" methods:

their malicious code works in memory from where
they elevate their privileges and start spreading into
the system. Abnormal activity like suspicious I/O or
privilege escalation can be detected using behavioral
analysis, which leverages ML/AI engines to look at
powered-on workloads.

VMware Live Cyber Recovery was recognized in the 2023 GIGAOM
Report and won an excellence Gold Awards for its contribution to
cybersecurity (Figure 1-5).

Figure 1-5. *VMware Live Cyber Recovery 2023 Excellence Award*

1.3.3 Common Use Cases for VMware Live Cyber Recovery

Choosing the right approach for your business continuity strategy or DR
plan can be complex. The decision involves factoring several inputs like
application criticality, business needs, TCO, scalability, reliability, and
assurance as well as simplicity in implementing a technology.

So now let's talk about some use cases that are enabled by VMware
Live Cyber Recovery.

Deploying a new DR solution: If you need to deploy a brand-new solution for your disaster recovery project, you may face a dilemma either to choose between a traditional approach or a cloud-powered solution. Finding a one-fits-all solution is hard and you may have to integrate multiple products from different vendors to address your needs. Another question is how you are going to address VMware workloads both on-premises and in the cloud if you have started to move them to VMware Cloud on AWS or in Google Cloud. As a SaaS-based managed service, VMware Live Cyber Recovery removes the need to deploy a secondary datacenter, which could be costly and time consuming when you need that capacity in a short time. Think about what happened during the pandemic where VDI infrastructure had to be delivered quickly to address remote workers. You just need to provision this failover capacity on demand and you are good to go. The scale-out file system is the core component that offers 15 minutes RPO as well as a modern approach to your DR testing with fast recovery time. VMware Live Cyber Recovery offers a way to implement a DR for both on-premises and VMware Cloud on AWS or GCVE production data center, so you don't have to implement two different approaches to address your multi-cloud project. One crucial factor is the familiarity with the tooling you are currently using to manage VMware workloads. VMware Live Cyber Recovery makes it easier to operate your DR environment as it keeps the workloads as they are (no change in the VM format) and you can still rely on your existing tooling without having to retrain your teams.

Modernizing (replacing or retiring an existing DR solution): One common use case is the modernization of your current DR solution by replacing it by VMware Live Cyber Recovery. If your current solution is too expensive, obsolete, or complex to manage and you can't add headcounts in your IT org, switching to a cloud DR can facilitate the evolution of your DR solution. One of the big challenges with DR is that you need to have an infrastructure ready to go in the event of a disaster, and this can often be an expensive proposition in terms of capital investment. With VMware

Live Cyber Recovery, you can run a small pilot light environment with the data replicated to the SCFS and then spin up additional workload nodes as needed to support your workloads as they are recovered. With the explosion of data growth, it is also hard to accommodate the datacenter to meet the needs of DR storage. VMware Live Cyber Recovery relies on the cloud file system, which provides scalability and on-demand capacity. If you want to get a faster recovery time, you can always use the Pilot Light mode for the recovery SDDC. With the scale-out file system, you can get low TCO and fast recovery times combined with a low RTO of 15 minutes that helps you to achieve regular non-disruptive testing of your plans for a higher confidence. In addition, the solution will help build an audit-ready DR through automated compliance check and workflows along with an integrated reporting of testing, failover, and failback operations.

Rapid ransomware recovery: Ransomware isn't going away; it is growing faster and faster. Ransomware attacks have risen by 13% in the last five years, with an average cost of $1.85 million per incident. By 2031, statistics predict a ransomware attack every two seconds. It requires investment at the company-wide level to implement a modern ransomware protection with a pragmatic approach from best practice training for all employees to a reliable and tested plan to recover data in case you do get attacked. VMware Live Cyber Recovery offers the best platform to address the ransomware recovery process with the following features:

- **Immutable and air-gapped recovery points**: These are the mandatory characteristics you should look for when choosing the best solution as recommended by Gartner.

- **Confident recovery from existential threats**: Think of implementing a NGAV that can address the complexity of modern attacks, which are undetectable by traditional antivirus solutions.

- **Quick recovery with guided automation and rapid recovery point validations**: Imagine you were hit by ransomware and have to face the daunting task of analyzing the snapshots and finding the encrypted ones. You would need to a workflow in place to guide you through the recovery process.

- **Simplified recovery operations with non-disruptive testing**: Recovering data when you don't have an isolated environment can be risky as it can spread the bad code into your production even further and make the damage worse.

1.3.4 What Makes VLCR Different?

VMware Cloud Disaster Recovery offers on-demand disaster recovery, delivered as an easy-to-use SaaS solution with cloud economics. It combines cost-efficient cloud storage with simple SaaS-based management to deliver IT resiliency at scale, through simple testing and orchestration of failover and failback plans. Customers benefit from a "pay when you need" failover capacity model for DR resources, while strengthening business resilience in the face of data loss threats such as ransomware.

On-demand DR/fast recovery: VMware Live Recovery offers fast recovery thanks to the instant power-on capabilities. Instant power-on is important regarding the pain point of selecting the right snapshot when doing a ransomware recovery. Oftentimes the first one is not the right one; with an iterative process to find the right candidate, instant power-on is a great time-savings feature.

The ability to have the Pilot Light instances within VMware Cloud on AWS SDDC to accelerate the recovery times and get a near zero RTO is really a plus. This means you can run a minimal number of resources without wasting a huge amount of money.

Ease of use: All VMware Cloud DR components, including the cloud storage/cloud site, are deployed, and managed by VMware in an AWS account that is dedicated to each tenant. VMware Cloud Disaster Recovery offers on-demand disaster recovery, delivered as an easy-to-use SaaS solution with cloud economics. It combines cost-efficient cloud storage with simple SaaS-based management to deliver IT resiliency at scale, through simple testing and orchestration of failover and failback plans. The ability to realize frequent and non-disruptive testing of recovery plans ensures highly predictable recovery objectives.

Low TCO and low environmental impact: Customers benefit from a "pay when you need" failover capacity model for DR resources while strengthening business resilience in the face of data loss threats such as ransomware. With the cost effectiveness and the low total cost of ownership with this cloud model, customers pay for capacity only when it's needed, taking advantage of very efficient cloud storage. And, finally, with the built-in failback capabilities, you only have to transfer over the WAN the actual deltas, as opposed to needing to transfer the entire backup.

Ransomware recovery: VMware Live Cyber Recovery is a great ransomware recovery platform with many capabilities as best practices to implement RWR. It provides deep snapshot history of hours, days, or even months and can recover all these snapshots without any RTO penalty. Backups are immutable by design as the system is air-gapped. VMware Cloud on AWS SDDC works very well as an IRE and it offers a great on-demand option to help save money. The IRE is a VMC SDDC preconfigured with a backup datastore. You can restore backups instantly into an SDDC without having to copy any data to it. You can also implement custom network isolation levels in the IRE based on the NSX-T Advanced Firewall feature. You can consider it as a "safe" place to spin up ransomware recovery VMs to prevent your production environment from seeing reinfection.

In the event you want to restore VMs before the bad guys infect the system, a differentiator is the file and level restore that can be used to recover VMs before the code is present and rehydrating more recent data from a more recent snapshot.

With VMware Live Cyber Recovery brings the opportunity to switch to the new paradigm of DRaaS and help build a more trustworthy and easier-to-use disaster recovery solution with modern technologies to cover the challenges of protecting your applications and business data.

1.4 Summary

In an overly changing IT landscape with demanding applications owners and critical business requirements over data protection, it is important to implement the right disaster recovery solution within the adequate well-documented Business Continuity Plan and DR Plan.

Ransomware adds another level of complexity and challenges when it comes to implementing the right disaster recovery approach and it needs special features, as stated by Gartner, like air-gapped and immutable storage.

In this Chapter you have learnt how VMware Live Cyber Recovery provides a simple and cost effective approach to implementing a DR solution with ransomware recovery capabilities. It uses a SaaS-based solution based on a scalable storage and on-demand compute/storage capacity in the cloud based on VMware Cloud on AWS. It offers business value and supports several deployment models and can protect both on-premises and cloud environments.

CHAPTER 2

Understanding VMware Live Cyber Recovery

This chapter provides an educational and pragmatic approach to the different components that make VMware Live Cyber Recovery. It starts by presenting the main building blocks of the solution and continues by providing a clear description of how to implement and integrate the whole DRaaS solution into your environment and start replicating and protecting workloads in the cloud.

2.1 Foundation of VMware Live Cyber Recovery

VMware Live Cyber Recovery is a service that was brought to market in 2020 as part of the acquisition of Datrium by VMware.

2.1.1 Introduction to DR as a Service

VMware Cloud Live Cyber Recovery is a SaaS-based service that helps customers optimize and streamline their DR solution by leveraging the cloud and automation of DR processes. It is a service provided by VMware

© Christophe Lombard 2024
C. Lombard, *Mastering VMware Cloud Disaster Recovery and Ransomware Resilience*,
https://doi.org/10.1007/979-8-8688-0829-6_2

that offers disaster recovery as a service (DRaaS) for on-premises vSphere, VMware Cloud on AWS, and Google Cloud VMware Engine (GCVE) workloads.

It regularly take snapshots and efficiently replicates the critical workloads to a scale-out file system (SCFS). The SCFS can store hundreds of recovery points with recovery point objectives (RPOs) as low as 30 minutes. This allows for recovery from a wide range of disasters, including ransomware.

Virtual machines can be recovered to a software-defined data center (SDDC) running in VMware Cloud on AWS.

VMware Cloud Live Cyber Recovery uses a SaaS Orchestrator to plan, coordinate, and automate the disaster recovery plan and make sure the replicated virtual machines are brought to the inventory and restarted in the recovery SDDC during a failover.

Additionally, VMware Cloud Live Cyber Recovery includes failback capabilities to return workloads to their original location once the disaster has been resolved. Designed for IT infrastructure professionals responsible for IT services and availability, it offers reliable, cost-effective, user-friendly disaster recovery with fast recovery capabilities.

VMware Live Cyber Recovery can protect virtual machines from an on-premises datacenter as well from an SDDCs in VMware Cloud on AWS or in Google Cloud VMware Engine[1].

The replication is managed through Protection Groups that specify both the frequency and retention of each snapshot. Each protected workload can be placed into a Protection Group based on certain criteria like naming or tags.

Recovery of the workloads and applications in the DR site is controlled by a Recovery Plan (RP) that defines the order in which virtual machines will be started, the resource pools to which they will be allocated, and the networking configuration.

---

[1] Google Cloud VMware Engine (GCVE) enables you to migrate or extend your on-premise VMware workloads to Google Cloud without refactoring the applications.

There is an option to test an RP using a temporary copy of the replicated data without interrupting the ongoing operations on the protected site.

It's a best practice to leverage multiple RPs to protect different applications based on certain criteria like type of environment, criticality, and business purposes. You can have one RP per application and a global RP that covers all the applications to be able to do a complete site failover. A continuous compliance check feature checks all recovery plans every 30 minutes, allowing customers to execute failover and failback confidently.

Failback is fully automated as well. Once the disaster is over, and all workloads have been restarted into the recovery SDDC, the system automatically sends back only the changed data to the source data center, minimizing egress charges.

VMware Cloud Live Cyber Recovery provides on-demand DR for all VMware workloads and recovery alternatives for ransomware attacks and other disasters.

2.1.2 VMware Live Cyber Recovery Features and Capabilities

VMware Cloud Live Cyber Recovery provides familiar features and functionality with enhanced workflows and capabilities to reduce the time to protection and limit the risk in case of a disaster.

- **On-demand DR environment**: One particular benefit is the ability to leverage an easy-to-use and on-demand disaster recovery site as a recovery site that is entirely managed by VMware based on VMware Cloud on AWS. The on-demand capability helps lower capital costs and makes it easier to protect more virtual machines faster.

- **Policy-based application-agnostic protection** eliminates the need for app-specific point solutions.

- **Automated orchestration** of site failover and failback with a single click reduces recovery times. This workflow makes creating, personalizing, and testing Recovery Plans a very easy process.

- **Frequent, non-disruptive testing** of recovery plans ensures highly predictable recovery objectives. Customers often do not test their DR plans; with this solution, it is very simple to launch a failover test for a sample of your applications or the entire datacenter.

- **Centralized management of Recovery Plans**: The concept of Recovery Plans simplifies the complexity of having to maintain manually runbooks and documentation related to DR.

- **VM-centric replication**: Live Cyber Recovery protects the virtual machines independently from storage (NFS, VMFS, VVOLs) and there is no modification in the VM format. Since there is no transformation to achieve when recovering a VM, the process is very fast.

- **Consistent operations**: Operating your DR environment on-premises and in the cloud is simplified using a centralized cloud management console called the SaaS Orchestrator. It facilitates specifying the perimeter of the protected environment as well as creating the relevant recovery strategy.

- **Cloud economics**: Lower DR costs from an on-demand data center in the public cloud

- **Low RPO**: RPOs as low as 15 minutes to minimize data loss and address the most critical needs

- **Instant restart**: You can benefit from a near zero RTO of any VMware workload from a cost-effective cloud-optimized storage. This not only helps accelerate recovery after a disaster but also facilitates the iteration during a ransomware recovery.

- **Low TCO**: VMware Cloud Live Cyber Recovery is a pure SaaS service with no hardware deployment on-premises and no hardware or software maintenance. Every component is completely managed by VMware including software patching and remote monitoring of cloud and on-premises components to avoid disruption into the DR process.

2.1.3 Integration with VMware Cloud on AWS

VMware Live Cyber Recovery is a SaaS-based service that leverages the Cloud (VMware cloud-based managed services) as well as VMware Cloud on AWS as a recovery DR site. VMware Cloud on AWS is a fully managed (by VMware) and jointly engineered service that brings VMware's enterprise-class, software-defined datacenter architecture to the AWS public cloud infrastructure.

VMware Live Cyber Recovery is an additional feature of VMware Cloud on AWS, which combines VMware's key compute, storage, and network virtualization products (VMware vSphere, VMware vSAN, and VMware NSX) with VMware vCenter Server management. These products are optimized to operate on an elastic, bare-metal AWS infrastructure. VMware Cloud on AWS and VMware vSphere deliver the same architecture and operational experience whether on-premises or in the cloud. See Figure 2-1.

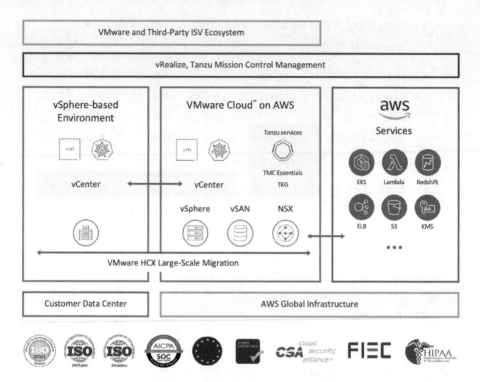

Figure 2-1. *VMware Cloud on AWS*

It provides an ability to rapidly power on and get the workloads running on to a VMware Cloud on AWS SDDC with a Pilot Light option for even faster RTO.

In the event of a disaster, VMware Live Cyber Recovery can provision VMware resources in the form of an SDDC in VMware Cloud on AWS. The stored replicas, which could be minutes old or even many years old, are instantly powered on from the scale-out cloud file system that is already "live mounted" directly to the SDDC, resulting in low RTO.

VMware Live Cyber Recovery expands VMware Cloud on AWS to provide managed disaster recovery, disaster avoidance, and non-disruptive testing capabilities to VMware customers without the need for a secondary site or complex configurations.

2.1.4 VMware Live Cyber Recovery Pricing and Billing

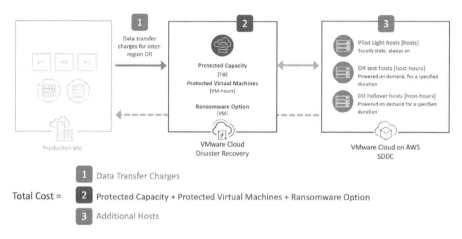

Figure 2-2. *VMware Live Cyber Recovery pricing model*

There are several VMware Cloud DR purchase options that you can choose from (also shown in Figure 2-2):

- **Protected capacity subscription**: Protected storage capacity is the sum of the logical (i.e., used) storage size, measured in Tebibytes (TiB), of your protected virtual machines and all the incremental snapshots you choose to replicate to and retain into the cloud file system. This can be purchased on a one-year or three-year subscription term. Subscriptions can be prepaid upfront or billed on a monthly cadence.

- **Protected VMs term subscriptions**: Protected virtual machines are the virtual machines being replicated using the service (regardless of whether the virtual machines are currently powered on in the recovery site). You can pay upfront or monthly for one-year or three-year subscriptions to protect individual VMs.

29

- **Pilot Light hosts** are the hosts for your Pilot Light configuration.

- **Additional DR failover hosts** are the additional hosts required to conduct DR failovers over the specified duration.

- **Additional DR test hosts** are the additional hosts required to conduct DR tests over the specified duration.

- **Data transfer charges** are only applicable for inter-region DR.

When protecting workloads running in the cloud, replication traffic is charged like any other egress traffic originated from the workload VMs in a protected customer SDDC.

NB   A minimum 10 TiB of protected capacity per- Orchestrator recovery region applies across a subscription region, regardless of usage.

After you purchase VMware Live Cyber Recovery term subscription SKUs, you need to apply your subscription to a VMware Cloud Services Organization. From a billing perspective, in a steady state, you only pay for the replicas stored in the scale-out cloud file system.

2.2 Architecture and Deployment

2.2.1 VMware Live Cyber Recovery Architecture

VMWare Live Recovery Building Blocks

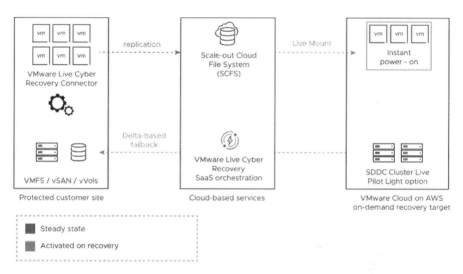

Figure 2-3. *VMware Live Cyber Recovery building blocks*

Each VMware Cloud Live Cyber Recovery deployment is divided into three parts (Figure 2-3):

- **Protected site**: This is the customer on-premises site or the Cloud SDDC that need to be protected (at the time of this writing, it can be either VMWare Cloud on AWS or Google Cloud VMware Engine[2]). It's important to mention that for workloads running in clusters on-premises, virtual machines can use any VMware datastore VSAN, NFS, VMFS, or VVOLS. There are certain

---

[2] GCVE is a GCP Cloud service that allows you to run VMware workloads in Google Cloud without having to refactor or rearchitect your applications.

unsupported ones like Raw Device Mappings RDMs[3], however. The protected sites hold the **Cyber Recovery Connectors**, which are virtual appliances installed in the vSphere environment to protect virtual machines.

- **Cloud-based services**: These essentially hold the **SaaS Orchestrator** and the **scale-out cloud file system** (SCFS) that store the replicated data securely and allow for an instant power on of virtual machines thanks to a live mount NFS feature.

- **Recovery target**: At **the time of a disaster, customers can spin up a new** VMware Cloud on AWS SDDC or use an existing one and recover their workloads. At the time of this writing, only VMware Cloud on AWS is supported as a recovery SDDC. There are plans to support additional solutions like Azure VMware Solution.

All VMware Live Recovery architecture components including the SaaS Orchestrator and the SCFS are deployed and managed by VMware in a dedicated AWS shadow account. Access to the managed service is done via a management console that enforces authentication and access controls in a unified way.

Cyber Recovery Connector

On the protected site, deploy the Cyber Recovery Connector and peer it with the vCenter where the virtual machines that need to be protected sit. The Cyber Recovery Connector enables the creation of secured copies of the data and a secured replication of the data to the cloud native storage.

---

[3] Raw device mapping is a mapping file that maps a LUN directly to a VM. In other words, RDM allows VMs to bypass VMFS—VMware's default storage management interface—and access the storage device directly.

Regardless of whether you are protecting an on-premises vSphere datacenter or a cloud SDDC like VMware Cloud on AWS, you will need to deploy a connector. See Figure 2-4.

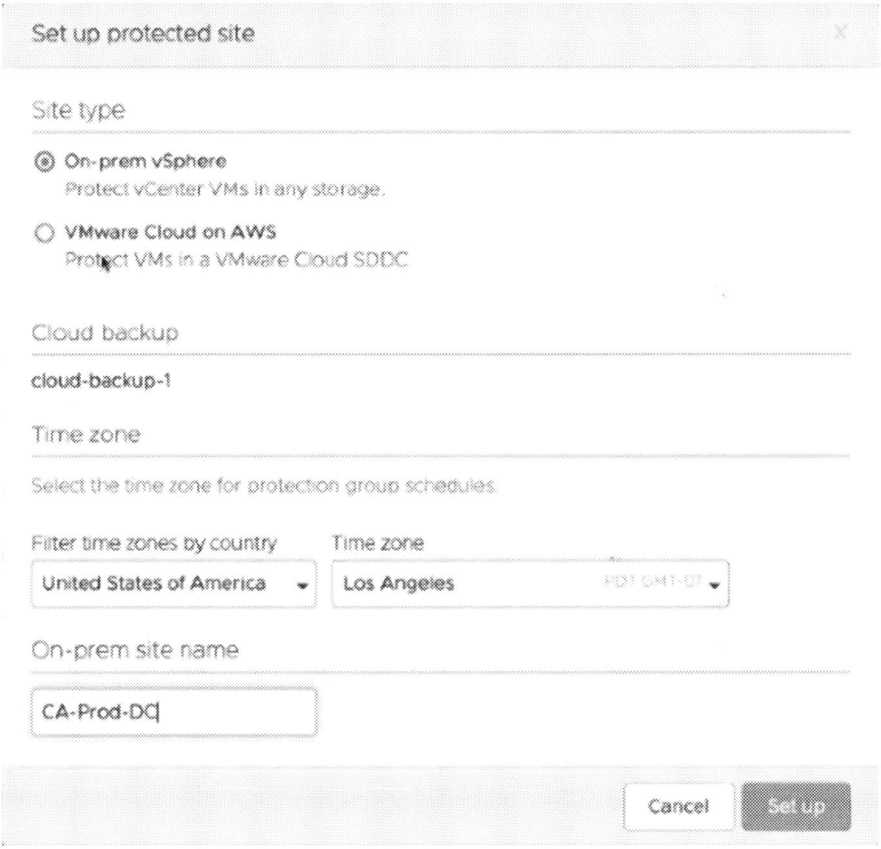

Figure 2-4. *Protected site creation*

A minimum of two connectors is recommended for high availability. The connector creates crash-consistent snapshots of the virtual machines' disk files. Customer data moves from the protected site to the scalable cloud file system thanks to the Cyber Recovery Connector.

The Cyber Recovery Connector always sits only on the source site that needs to be protected. In a steady state, this is all you need to have in place.

VMware is responsible for the ongoing upgrade of the orchestrators deployed in your environment.

VMware Live Cyber Recovery leverages VADP to snapshot the virtual machines.

The Cyber Recovery Connector works similarly to most VADP-capable backup software, so the workflow looks like this:

1. It makes a snapshot of the source VM. This stops all data changes to the VMDK files and redirects the writes to the log files.

2. It uses changed block tracking (CBT) to figure out which blocks in the VMDKs have changed since the last snapshot.

3. It uses VADP to read the changed blocks from the VMDKs, then compresses/encrypts/deduplicates this data in the memory of the Cyber Recovery Connector virtual appliance, and it's transmitted up to the SCFS.

4. Once it has read all the changed blocks from the VMDKs, it removes the snapshot from the source VM. This causes the source vCenter Server/ESXi hosts to take the data from the log files and apply it to the VMDK files.

A couple of additional points:

1. No deduplication is done within the Cyber Recovery Connector. The data is deduplicated once it is in the SCFS (roughly on a 12-hour cycle). This is also when sizes of data will show up in the UI. The solution does not expose the deduplication impact on the underlying storage.

2.   The first snapshot will essentially be a full copy
     of the VM. From that point, as long as the VADP
     structure is intact, then CBT can be exploited for
     delta changes.

3.   When the changes are replicated to the SCFS, there
     is a process similar to a synthetic full management
     such that the snapshots in SCFS are independent
     from each other and represent a complete PIT
     image of the virtual machines.

Scale-Out Cloud File System

The SCFS is a log structured file system with the intention of providing
high IO but leveraging a highly scalable type of storage as a back end. It
consists of a front-end caching system running on EC2 instances and a
cloud backend to store the data based on Amazon S3.

Once copied to the SCFS, the backups are encrypted at rest and stored
in native vSphere VM format. Data on the SCFS is optimized, compressed,
and cataloged.

It's important to mention that there is no media server and catalog that
could potentially be exposed to attackers.

The cloud backup is immutable and air-gapped. Data is never
overwritten and cannot be accessed, browsed, or changed.

As mentioned, during a failover or a test, the SCFS is exported as an
NFS mount to the hosts that are deployed in the recovery SDDC. Nothing
is really on it unless you initiate a recovery operation whether it's a DR
test or ransomware recovery or an actual failover. This process allows
for automatically starting the snapshots and gets the workloads back to
production.

Regardless of the option you pick, the SCFS and the VMware Cloud on
AWS recovery SDDC used will reside in the same AWS AZ. This helps with
speed as the data is much more local to the SDDC.

When you protect a VMware Cloud on AWS SDDC, you must select a different AZ or region because if the AZ goes down, you would be stuck since your DR would be in the same AZ!

VCDR knows this and forces you to pick a different area, as shown in Figure 2-5.

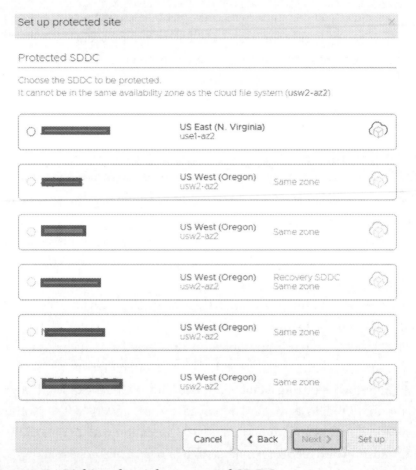

Figure 2-5. *Picking the right protected SDDC*

In this example, the SCFS is in usw2-az2 so you can't protect any of the VMC SDDCs in that region. As a result, only the top one is available to be used as a protected site.

SaaS Orchestrator

The SaaS Orchestrator is made of a web-based interface on which you can log in to manage all the aspects of your disaster and ransomware recovery strategies.

It is a DR orchestration service that runs in AWS and executes DR plans from new or old replicas. The role of the SaaS Orchestrator is also to provision and monitor SDDCs in VMware Cloud on AWS.

The SaaS orchestrator handles the following tasks:

- Creation of recovery SDDCs

- Establishing communication from the cloud Cyber Recovery Connector to the SaaS Orchestrator to manage/execute backup schedules

- Mounting the NFS volume during a test or actual failover

- Initiating the storage vMotion to local storage into the recovery SDDC VSAN storage

- Failback of VMs back to the protected site

- Facilitate exports of activity and reports

The SaaS Orchestrator automatically checks your plan for health and compliance every 30 minutes, so you can be confident your DR plan is going to work when you need it.

If you want to get protected quickly or want to do a pilot, typically the SaaS Orchestrator can be deployed in an hour.

Recovery Target

The recovery target is where the workload is brought back to. On a test, or when a disaster event or a ransomware attack happens, customers can recover their VMs to VMware Cloud on AWS using their pre-tested DR plans with just a few clicks from the UI.

VMware Live Cyber Recovery supports VMware Cloud on AWS 2-host clusters on i4i.metal, or i3-en.metal for Pilot Light failover environments.

New SDDC spin-up on average is about 90 minutes, but it really depends on various factors and the underlying AWS infrastructure. When SDDC is spun up, you get a live mount datastore from which the production workload can start working.

When production is back, you can do a failback. VMware Live Cyber Recovery supports failbacks and they are delta-based failbacks. It only moves the base or delta at the source site and it helps reduce the amount of data that gets transferred.

The solution is all VMware managed, including all the underlying infrastructure such as cloud native storage, the compute instances needed to run the SaaS Orchestrator, and the Cyber Recovery Connector.

2.2.2 Deployment Models and Considerations

Recovery Time Objectives (RTO)

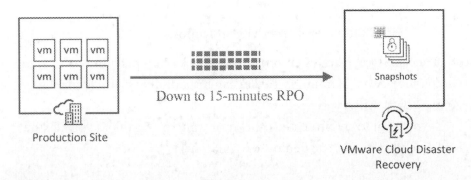

Figure 2-6. *Recovery Time Objectives*

VMware Live Cyber Recovery offers 15 minutes minimum RPO. This is possible through the implementation of a high frequency snapshot that leverages LWD (lightweight delta) instead of VADP for backup. LWD offers less performance impact because there is no VM stun during the snapshot process and a lower RPO. See Figure 2-6.

Deployment Models

Before deploying VMware Live Cyber Recovery, you must keep in mind the following considerations about the different sites:

- Protected sites
- Backup sites
- Recovery site

Protected sites: Protected sites encompasses vCenter Servers, protection groups, and Recovery Plans. A protected site (on-premises vSphere or an SDDC in the cloud in AWS or GCP) includes vCenter Servers which contain the workloads that need to be replicated.

Please note that one vCenter Server can only be registered to one protected site. However, one protected site can protect multiple vCenter servers. Each vCenter Server can hold multiple protection groups and recovery plans. The protected sites can be of three different types, as shown in Table 2-1.

Table 2-1. *Protected Site Types*

Scenario	Description	RPO	RTO	VM max
On-prem SCFS VMC	On-premises vSphere environment (check the version compatibility on the interoperability matrix)	15+ min	Near zero with Pilot Light	Up to 6000 per region
VMC SCFS VMC	VMware Cloud on AWS SDDC (one connector per vCenter) (check the version compatibility on the interoperability matrix)	15+ min	Near zero with Pilot Light	Up to 6000 per region
GCVE SCFS VMC	Google Cloud VMware Engine (check the version compatibility on the interoperability matrix)	15+ min	Near zero with Pilot Light	Up to 6000 per region

NB   When protecting an SDDC using VMware Live Cyber Recovery, the recovery SDDC and VMware Live Cyber Recovery deployment must be in the same CSP organization as the protected SDDC. You can't protect SDDC in a different organization as the one used by VLCR.

Each protected site holds at least one VLCR connector that replicates snapshots to the cloud file system by applying the backup policy defined in the protection group.

It's best practice to deploy at least two connectors per protected site.

Backup Sites: A backup site is the cloud backup where the replicated virtual machines are saved. You can choose to deploy additional backup sites to have separate failure domains, additional recovery SDDCs, and increase the total maximum capacity.

There is a one-to-one relationship between the SCFS and the recovery SDDC, meaning that you cannot attach multiple cloud storage to a single recovery SDDC. See Figure 2-7.

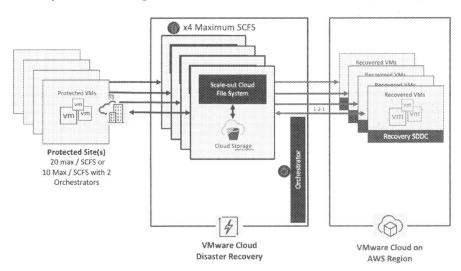

Figure 2-7. *Backup sites*

This also means that if you want to protect multiple virtual machines from multiple sites and recover them to the same SDDC, make sure you save them on the same cloud file system.

Recovery site: VMware Live Cyber Recovery provides two deployment methods:

- **On-demand (also known as "just in time") deployment**: Since there's no need to have any hosts on VMware Cloud on AWS, it's possible to spin up a brand new SDDC and instantly power on the stored backup VMs at any time of your choice without having to rehydrate any data. This is called a "live mount."

- **Pilot Light deployment**: Depending on your DR goals, the other option is Pilot Light; that is, to maintain a two-node SDDC footprint you always leave on and scale up as needed. The little-to-no SDDC footprint is really what will drive those steady state infrastructure costs much lower. You can add nodes/clusters to the two-host pilot light cluster at the time of recovery or during a failover test. You can scale back down to a two-host cluster by removing additional recovery hosts/clusters after the outage has passed. For an illustration of the pilot light option refer to Figure 2-8.

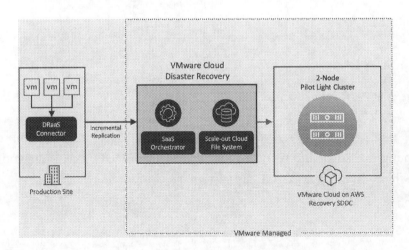

Figure 2-8. *Two-node Pilot Light recovery SDDC*

Considerations When Deploying and Configuring VMware LCR

Choosing an availability zone for recovery is one of the most important design decisions. To align to your compliance constraints or your DR strategy requirements, you must select the right AWS availability zone (AZ) for your backups before deploying the cloud file system.

One important factor to consider is that all cloud file systems and all recovery SDDCs must reside in the same AZ inside one AWS region. See Figure 2-9.

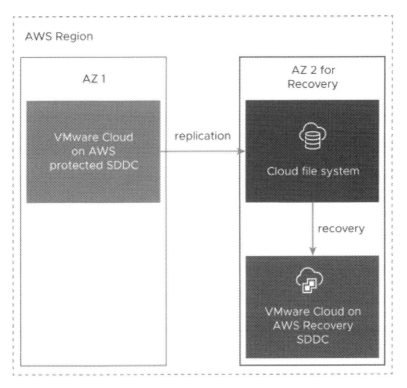

Figure 2-9. *Availability zones selection for VLCR*

Limitation with High Frequency Snapshots

With VMware Live Cyber Recovery, you can achieve 15 minutes RPO when you create a protection group by leveraging high-frequency snapshots. However, there are some caveats to know when using high frequency snapshots. Let's have a look at them.

If you plan to back up a VM with a third-party backup solution while it is protected using a high-frequency snapshot, there might be potential disruptions if the solution uses VMware APIs for Data Protection (VDAP). When the third-party backup solution creates or deletes a VADP backup at the same time VMware Live Cyber Recovery replicates a high-frequency snapshot, this snapshot task pauses and retries after a few seconds. VMware Live Cyber Recovery will continue the snapshot replication from the point of interruption.

If you plan to use VMware HCX together with the high-frequency snapshot, you cannot perform a bulk migration or a replication assisted vMotion (RAV).

It's not possible to protect VMs with vSphere encryption enabled.

SCFS to Recovery SDDC Connectivity

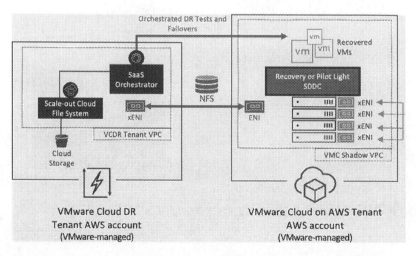

Figure 2-10. *Connectivity between scalable filesystem and the recovery SDDC*

In Figure 2-10, the left rectangle is the VMware Live Cyber Recovery shadow account virtual private cloud (VPC)[4] and the right rectangle is the VMC AWS shadow account[5]/VPC. When VMware Live Cyber Recovery is attached to an SDDC, two new dedicated ENIs are created in the VMC VPC: one for data path traffic (NFS) and the other for management traffic (not shown in the picture).

These blue ENIs are directly attached to SCFS instances as xENIs and don't contend with the gray xENIs in the picture. The gray xENIs are used for connectivity to a customer-linked account/VPC that is not shown in the diagram. Unlike VCDR traffic, the traffic to the customer-linked VPC flows over NSX Edge. VCDR traffic and linked customer VPC traffic don't contend for the same resources.

Standard-Frequency Snapshots and VADP

VMware Live Cyber Recovery and other VMware APIs for data protection (VADP) backup products can coexist as long as both products aren't trying to create snapshots at the same time.

There are certain cases that can conflict:

- If a VM is being backed up by another backup solution, and VMware Live Cyber Recovery starts a snapshot of the same VM after the other backup software started the backup, then the VMware Live Cyber Recovery snapshot might fail if the backup software finishes the backup before finishing replication of the VMware Live Cyber Recovery snapshot. In this case, even though the snapshot failed, the next scheduled snapshot will resume from where it failed.

---

[4] VPC: Virtual private cloud is an AWS network construct where you can deploy missing text

[5] Lacks explanation

- If a VM snapshot is being replicated by VMware Live
  Cyber Recovery, and another backup solution (non-
  VMware Live Cyber Recovery) starts a backup of the
  same VM after VMware Live Cyber Recovery started
  replication, then the backup might fail if VMware Live
  Cyber Recovery finishes the replication of snapshot
  before the backup software finishes the backup. See
  Figure 2-11.

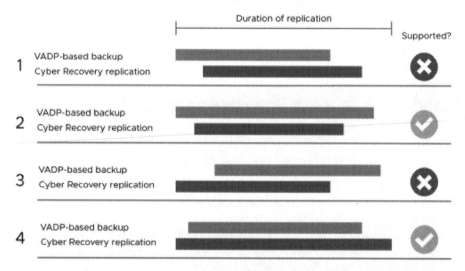

Figure 2-11. *VADP and Cyber Recovery replication coexistence*

For example, if VCDR is configured to take a daily snapshot at 10:00
pm, the customer should adjust their other backup product so that it
does its daily backup at 1:00 am (as an example). If both VCDR and the
other backup product were to take a snapshot at 10:00pm, they could
interfere with each other and one (or both) of them will fail their backup/
snapshot job.

Interconnection with VMware LCR

By default, the SaaS Orchestrator leverages internet access to replicate the data. If you want to use a more secure, reliable, and fast connectivity option between your protected sites and VMware Liver Cyber Recovery scalable cloud file system, you can leverage a private network connection.

For on-premises sites, it is possible to leverage AWS Direct Connect either with a private VIF or a public VIF. AWS Direct Connect provides a dedicated low latency private connection between your on-premises data center and AWS services. You can order it from your AWS account. For connections over DX, you must reserve a /26 CIDR block from your company's private IP network schema dedicated to the replication traffic.

For VMware Cloud on AWS protected SDDCs, VMware Transit Connect can provide high-bandwidth, low-latency connections between your protected SDDCs and VMware Live Cyber Recovery.

Direct Connect Public VIF is shown in Figure 2-12.

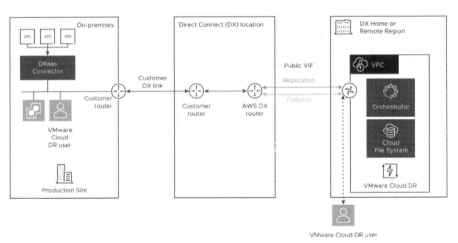

Figure 2-12. *Direct Connect Public VIF*

In that case, create a public VIF that will give you a direct access to public service IPs in AWS including the public IP addresses of VMware LCR.

Direct Connect Private VIF is shown in Figure 2-13.

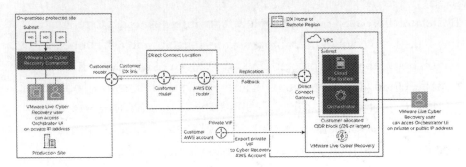

Figure 2-13. *Direct Connect Private VIF*

This is used when you want to interconnect your on-premises data center to VLCR through private IP addresses of the AWS Virtual Private Cloud. When you configure the connection, and create the private VIF, make sure you grab the right AWS shadow account ID from the VLCR console.

Select the /26 CIDR block within your company's private IP network scheme and make sure it does not overlap with other allocated CIDR blocks within your routed on-premises networks.

NB   The 172.30.0.0/26 subnet cannot be used because it is reserved by VMware Live Cyber Recovery internal networking.

To setup the private network connection, go to the **Settings** Menu and select **Set Up Private Connection** where you must enter the reserved CIDR block from your company's private network. See an illustration on how to configure a private CIDR block for replication in Figure 2-14.

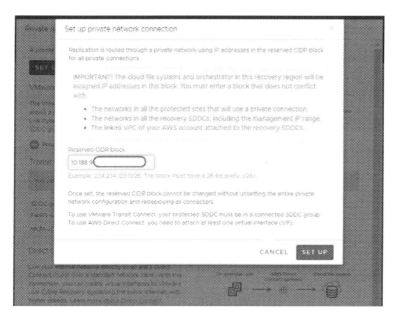

Figure 2-14. *Set up a private network connection*

You must also select an appropriate and valid autonomous system number (ASN) number for the connectivity to be established. By default, VLCR uses the ASN number 64512 and cannot be used by the on-premises side. Have a look at Figure 2-15 for a clearer view on how the Private VIFs are interconnected.

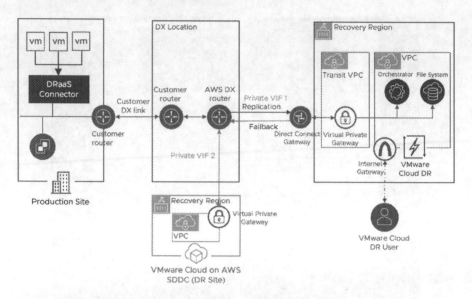

Figure 2-15. *Direct Connect with two private VIFs*

As you can see in **Figure 2-15**, you can use two logical private VIFs inside your Direct Connect physical connection, one to attach your on-premises data center to the VLCR recovery region and one for the recovery SDDC of VMware Cloud on AWS.

Transit Connect: To avoid going over the internet, the third option is to use a **Transit Connect**. It offers a secure dedicated private connection to provide high bandwidth, low-latency connections between the protected SDDC and VMware Live Cyber Recovery.

This option is only available when you protect a VMware Cloud on AWS SDDC. In this case, you must create an SDDC group. VMware Transit Connect uses an AWS Transit Gateway component to provide a dedicated, high bandwidth connectivity between SDDCs within a single region or across regions.

As for Direct Connect, the first step prior to using Transit Connect is to set up a /26 CIDR block for the connection. This CIDR block is used to route all replication traffic to the cloud file system in this reserved block.

Be aware that it incurs additional charges. AWS charges $0.02/GB for cross-regional traffic between EC2 instances in different regions (even without Direct Connect).

The short story is that for region-to-region replication, VLCR replication charges will be combined with all other SDDC egress charges and will appear on the general VMC bill.

While not strictly guaranteed by AWS, for most source/destination region pairs, the replication traffic stays on the AWS backbone with a very good bandwidth.

For AZ-to-AZ initial release, the network path is the same as for region-to-region with the same charges applied.

To configure a private connection using Transit Connect, follow these steps:

- Select Settings and click Private Network Connection.

- In the Private Network Connection, under Transit Connect SDDC groups, click Connect.

- After the group and SDDCs are connected, the Connection to VMware Live Cyber Recovery column shows the group's connection status as Available. Click Close. See Figure 2-16.

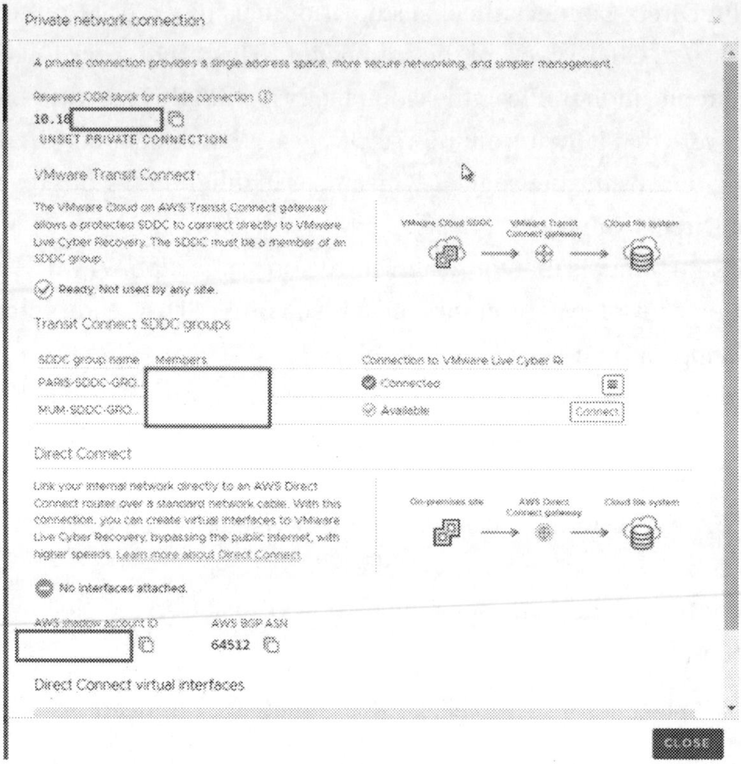

Figure 2-16. *Transit Connect settings*

2.2.3 Setting Up a DR Environment

To achieve your DR strategy objectives when building the VMware Live Cyber Recovery solution, you should start by deploying the main components:

- The SaaS Orchestrator

- The SCFS

- The Cyber Recovery Connector

Once they have been deployed, you will be able to configure the remaining elements that are more instrumental to the DR strategy:

- The protected sites

- The protection groups

- The DR plans

There are keys stages to follow to successfully deploy VMware Live Cyber Recovery. Begin protecting critical workloads and start testing the DR strategy:

1. Apply a subscription.

2. Activate a region.

3. Deploy the Cloud file systems and SaaS Orchestrator.

4. Restrict access to the service.

5. Register protected sites.

6. Create protection groups.

7. Define DR Plans.

8. Deploy a recovery site.

Let's have a look at them in more detail.

Apply a Subscription

After your purchase, VMware Cloud Services will send an email to the email address associated with your account that contains an invite link to VMware Cloud Services, so you can apply these subscriptions to your organization.

Once the order is processed, your VMware Live Cyber Recovery subscription is created and term billing begins.

It can take up to 6 hours after activation for subscriptions to become available in the VMware Live Cyber Recovery Global Console. You can, however, see the subscription in the VMware Cloud Services console.

Activate Region and SaaS Orchestrator

Before you starting using VMware Live Recovery, you need to activate the desired region and deploy both the SaaS Orchestrator and the SCFS.

When you activate a recovery region, you establish the Orchestrator and cloud file system on VMware Cloud on AWS. The recovery region is where you deploy recovery SDDCs, run failover recovery plans, and replicate snapshots to the cloud file system using protection groups.

To activate a VMware Live Cyber Recovery Region, you must have Global Console Admin access in the roles for VMware Cloud DR I&AM.

Any "new" clients with CSP access will have Global Console Admin access by default.

Clients with existing CSP deployments may not have access, and if they are not authorized to deploy, this setting should be checked. See Figure 2-17.

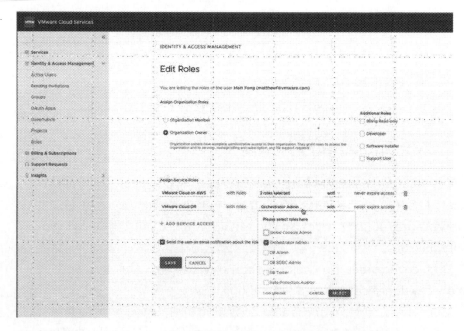

Figure 2-17. *Role's creation in the Cloud Services portal*

Once you have the right role, you can go to the Cloud console and select **Set up Cyber Recovery Region**. The selected region is for the initial Orchestrator to be deployed in. See Figure 2-18.

Figure 2-18. *Set up a Cyber Recovery region*

In the next step, select the AWS region where to deploy the scalable file system. See Figure 2-19.

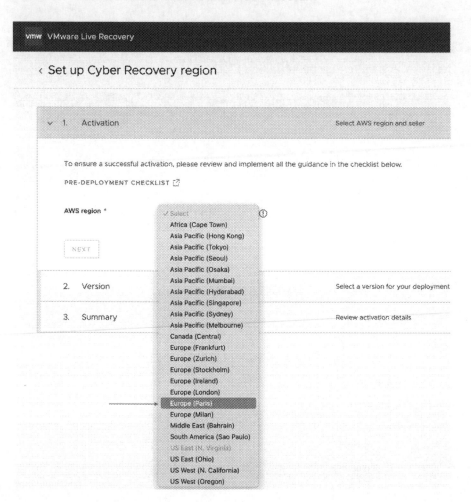

Figure 2-19. *Set up an AWS region*

Once it has been selected, the region is activated and lands into a more global regional deployment.

Pick the deployment version that fits your needs. It is always better to select the last version of the service. See Figure 2-20.

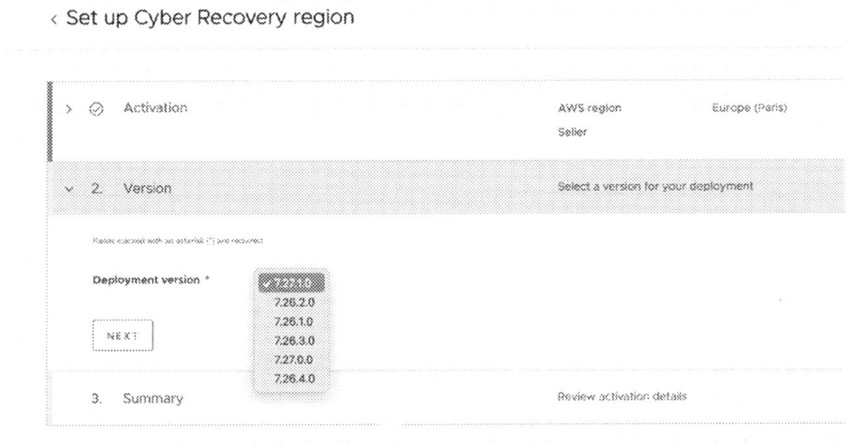

< Set up Cyber Recovery region

Figure 2-20. *Version selection for cyber recovery region*

You are presented with a recap of the options selection for the Cyber Recovery region creation in Figure 2-21.

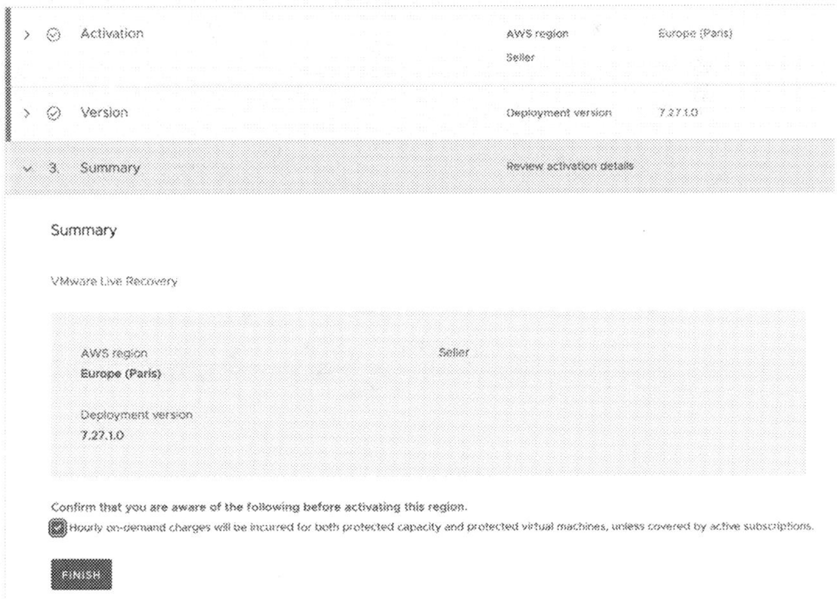

Figure 2-21. *Confirmation screen for Cyber Recovery region creation*

Confirm the hourly on-demand charges that can be incurred for both capacity and protected virtual machines if not covered by active subscriptions.

Generate an API Token

Once the region has been activated, and before using the service, you need to create an **API token** so that the VMware Live Cyber Recovery service can interact with the VMware Cloud on AWS service so that when there is an event, it can spin up an SDDC and recover the VM.

The first thing to validate before creating the API token is to check that the user has the proper roles with the right scope of permissions for both the organization and service roles.

To create an API token, you must log into your VMware Cloud Portal and select your account. See Figure 2-22.

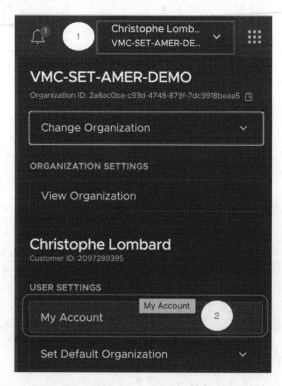

Figure 2-22. *My Account option in the CSP Portal*

Select API Tokens from the sub menu and click Generate API Token.
An example of the creation of an API token is a follow:

- Enter a token name: VCDR

- Choose the token TTL: 12 months (maximum lifespan
  is 60 months)

- Select Org Owner Role for the organization role

- Pick the Service Roles: Administrator and NSX
  Cloud Admin

NB   VMware Live Cyber Recovery doesn't tell you that you don't
have the right permission. **Administrator** and **NSX Cloud Admin**
service roles are mandatory.

It is a best practice to create a generic user account to make sure the
account is not deleted because the deletion will disable the API token. The
replication will continue; however, if the customer wants to failover, you
will start running into issues.

Using multi-factor authentication (MFA) with API tokens is currently
not supported with VMware Cloud DR.

The maximum lifespan of a token is 60 months. If you do not
regenerate a new token when the old one expires, the service will
experience failures of certain features. The best practice is to create an API
token with the longest time to live (TTL) possible in order to avoid service
interruption. Select to send email reminders to be able to be informed
when the API token is going to expire.

Once you have created a new API token, you can paste it in the
VMware Live Cyber Recovery Console to finish the configuration.

The menu to configure it is available from the Quick Setup menu, as
shown in Figure 2-23.

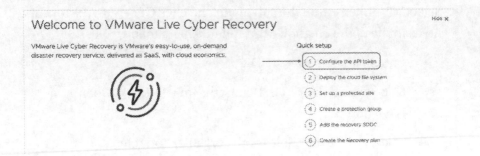

Figure 2-23. *Quick Setup menu*

Or you can go through the Settings accessible on the left navigation, as shown in Figures 2-24 and 2-25.

Figure 2-24. *API token settings*

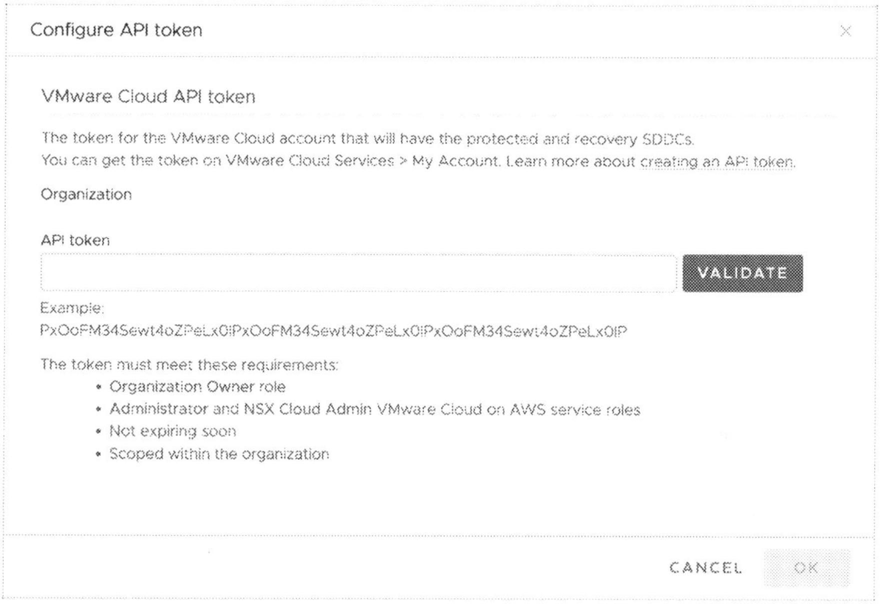

Figure 2-25. *API token configuration*

Paste your API token in the API Token field. Once the validation is complete, you can click OK to finish the process.

If after a deployment you need to update the API token it's possible to change the API Token and it's a very easy process.

Configure Access to the Service

To comply with your security requirements or for compliance reasons like PCI DSS, you may have to restrict access to the service from specific IP addresses. This is possible by implementing access lists that allows you to

- Restrict access from the Cyber Recovery Connector to the cloud-based services (SCFS and SaaS Orchestrator).

- Control which users can access the VMware Cloud Cyber Recovery UI.

- Harden your environment for PCI DSS requirements.

There are two access lists that can be implemented:

- **Connector Access list**: A list of Cyber Recovery Connector IP addresses that can access the Cloud Orchestrator.

- **Management Access List**: A list of public IP addresses that are allowed to access the VMware Live Cyber Recovery UI.

NB   You can add a maximum of 14 IP addresses total between both access lists.

To implement the access lists, follow this procedure:

1. From the left navigation, select **Settings**.

2. Click the **Security and compliance** button.

3. In the **Security and compliance** dialog box, select the **Use access list** option. See Figure 2-26.

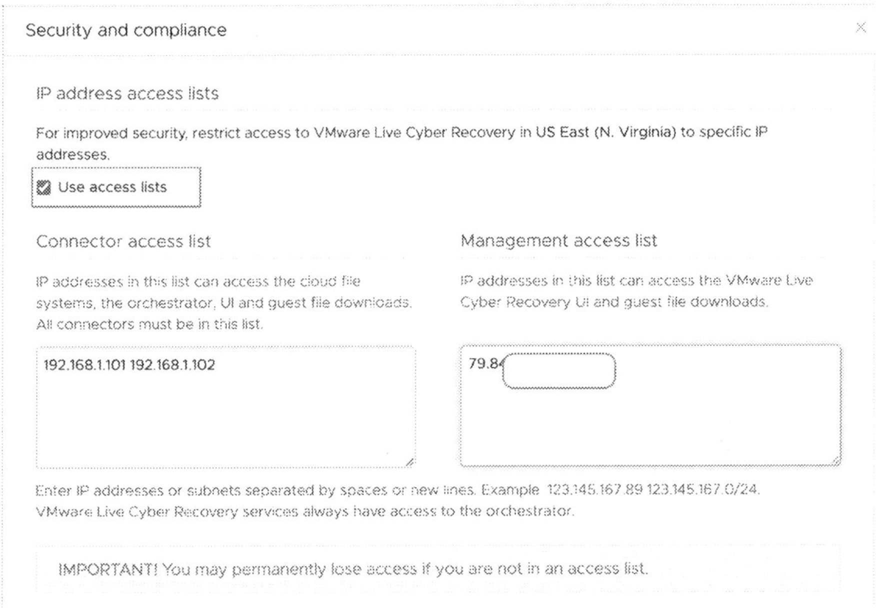

Figure 2-26. *Security and Compliance settings*

Deploy the Scalable Cloud File System

The SCFS is mandatory as it enables storage capacity for the protected virtual machines. The SCFS is a log structured file system with the intention to provide high IO but leveraging the S3 type of storage as a back end, front-caching system running on an EC2 instance.

VMware Live Cyber Recovery replicates snapshots to the cloud file system for backup. These snapshots are later used for failover operations to a recovery SDDC.

Before deploying the SCFS, you need to decide where to deploy it.

- If you want to protect a VMware Cloud on AWS SDDC, the cloud file system must be in a different AZ from the SDDC you want to protect.

- In the inverse, if a customer already has an SDDC
  deployed that they want to use as a recovery target,
  then the cloud file system must be in the same AZ as
  the SDDC that you want to use for recovery.

- If the protected SDDC is in another region, you don't
  care what AZ the SCFS is deployed into.

To deploy the cloud file system, you can select option 2, **Deploy the cloud file system** from the Quick Setup menu. Click **Deploy cloud file system** to start the configuration. See Figure 2-27.

Figure 2-27. *Cloud File Systems deployment menu*

1. From the pop-up configuration menu, select the
   AWS AZ that matches the VLCR service location that
   you have selected. If you want to protect workloads
   on an SDDC, choose an AZ that is different than the
   AZ where your protected SDDCs are deployed. If a
   cloud file system has already been deployed, then
   the recovery AZ is already selected.

2. Name the file system to something that is
   meaningful.

3. Click Deploy to complete the configuration. See
   Figure 2-28.

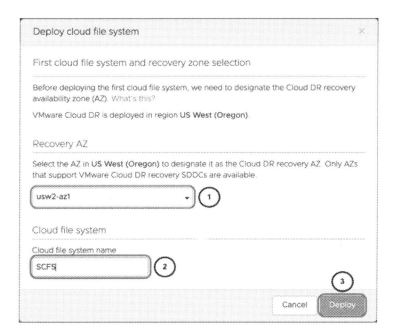

Figure 2-28. *Deploy cloud file system options*

During the deployment, the screen in Figure 2-29 will display.

Figure 2-29. *SCFS deployment process in motion*

You must wait for the SCFS to be deployed before you can continue configuring a protected site. It takes **around 15 minutes to deploy the SCFS**.

Once you have an **API token** and **SCFS** deployed, you can implement your DR by registering protected sites and start creating Protection Groups for protection of virtual machines.

2.2.4 Setting Up My Protected Sites

Once the main components like the SCFS have been deployed, it is time to implement the DR strategy, which means deploying the Cyber Recovery Connectors and start replicating your first virtual machines.

This starts by setting up your protected sites.

Consideration with Protected Sites

To set up a VMware Live Cyber Recovery Site, you need to first define your protected site: it could be on-premises vSphere or an existing VMware Cloud on AWS or GCVE SDDC. The most common is on-premises. You can set up a protected SDDC on one AWS region and perform backup and recovery in the same (intra-region DR) or in a different AWS region (inter-region DR). With intra-region DR, you can only protect an SDDC that resides in a different availability zone than the cloud file system.

New protected sites are created from the Orchestrator UI. Just give it a unique name and assign it a time zone for scheduling.

On-premise vSphere: Before configuring the on-premises environment, note the network requirements for the Cyber Recovery Connector.

To create the protected site for on-premises vSphere, follow this procedure:

1. In the VMware Cloud Disaster Recovery UI, click Sites and select **Protected sites**.

2. Click the **Set up protected site** button in the upper right corner.

3. In the Setup protected site dialog box, under Site types select **On-premises site**.

4. Under Cloud backup, select a cloud file system to use for backups from the protected SDDC. If a cloud file system is already deployed, then that cloud file system is selected by default.

5. Under Connection to cloud, select either **Use public internet** (including a public VIF, if you have configured Direct Connect on the site) or **Use Direct Connect with private VIF**.

6. Select a time zone from the drop-down menu, and then click the button on the right to set the time zone for the protected site.

7. Enter a name for the protected site.

8. Click **Setup**. See Figure 2-30.

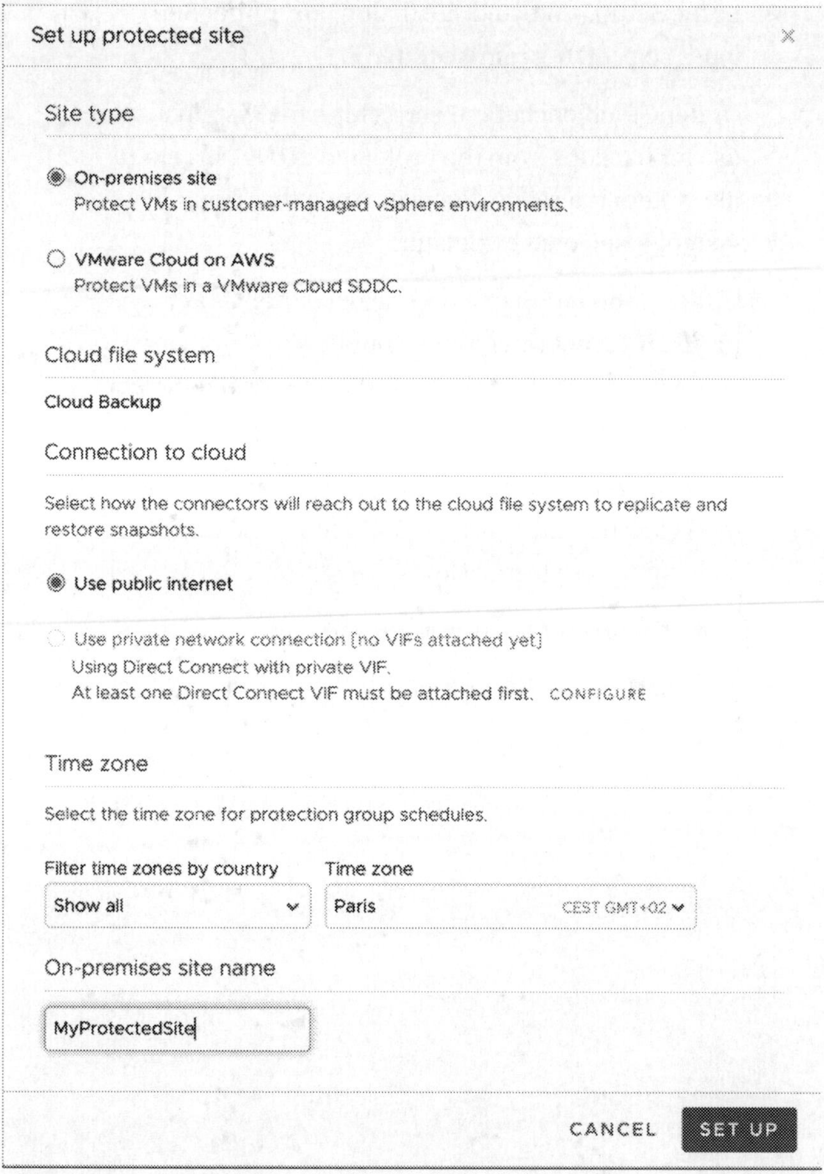

Set up protected site   ×

Site type

◉ **On-premises site**
   Protect VMs in customer-managed vSphere environments.

○ **VMware Cloud on AWS**
   Protect VMs in a VMware Cloud SDDC.

Cloud file system

Cloud Backup

Connection to cloud

Select how the connectors will reach out to the cloud file system to replicate and restore snapshots.

◉ **Use public internet**

○ Use private network connection (no VIFs attached yet)
   Using Direct Connect with private VIF.
   At least one Direct Connect VIF must be attached first.   CONFIGURE

Time zone

Select the time zone for protection group schedules.

Filter time zones by country   Time zone
[Show all   ⌄]   [Paris   CEST GMT+02 ⌄]

On-premises site name

[MyProtectedSite|]

                                        CANCEL   [SET UP]

Figure 2-30. *Protected site configuration*

VMware Cloud on AWS SDDC

1. From the left navigation, select Protected sites.

2. Click the Set up protected site button. See Figure 2-31.

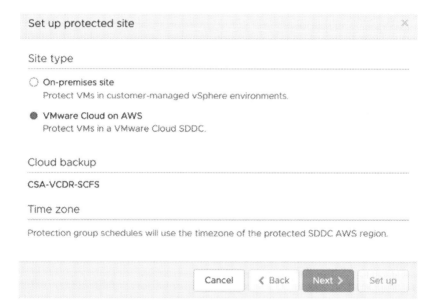

Figure 2-31. *Protected site selection*

3. In the Setup protected site dialog box, under Site types select **VMware Cloud on AWS**.

4. Under Cloud backup, select a cloud file system to use for replicating snapshots from the protected SDDC. If there is already one cloud file system deployed, then it is selected. Click **Next**.

On the next page under **Protected SDDC**, select an existing SDDC to protect. The list of SDDCs in your organization are then displayed. You can see that only the SDDC that is in a different AZ from the SCFS can be used. In Figure 2-32, I picked the SDDC in the US East North Virginia region.

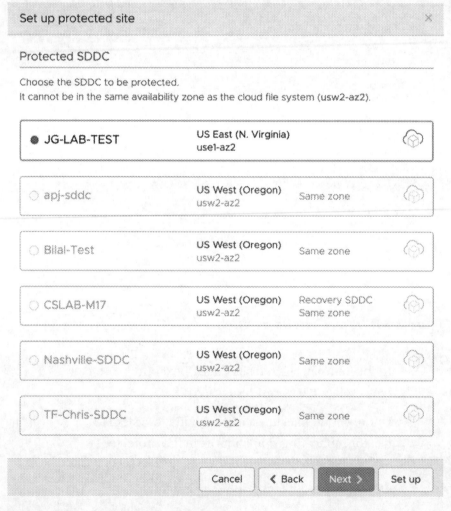

Figure 2-32. Select protected SDDC

The UI indicates the AWS region and availability zone for each SDDC. To perform replication and recovery operations across regions, select an SDDC that is in a different region than the recovery SDDC.

On the next page, under Network connection, select either **Use public internet** or **Use private network connection**, as shown in Figure 2-33.

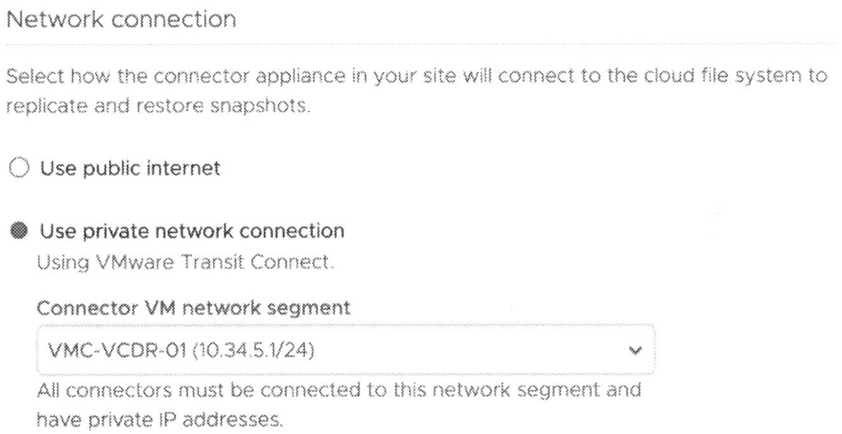

Network connection

Select how the connector appliance in your site will connect to the cloud file system to replicate and restore snapshots.

○ Use public internet

● Use private network connection
Using VMware Transit Connect.

Connector VM network segment

VMC-VCDR-01 (10.34.5.1/24)   ⌄

All connectors must be connected to this network segment and have private IP addresses.

Figure 2-33. *Protected site selection – Use private connection*

If you select **Use private connection**, a dedicated secure private connection will be set up through a VMware Transit Connect. To use VMware Transit Connect, your SDDC must be connected to an SDDC Group created in advance and a unique /26 CIDR block has to be chosen.

The connector is a VM that has to be deployed on a compute segment in the SDDC.

Under Initial firewall configuration, you are presented with two choices: to manually create the gateway firewall rules or let the system automatically add the right rules for you (recommended). See Figure 2-34.

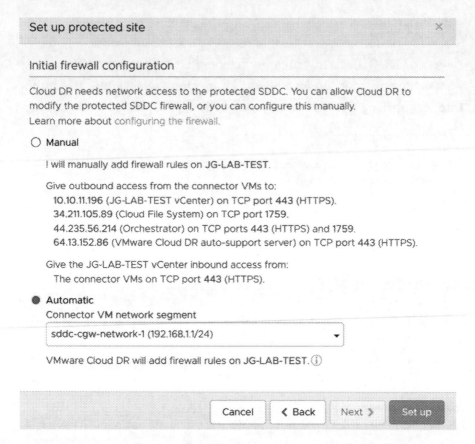

Figure 2-34. *Setting up protected SDDC - initial firewall configuration*

Select one of the options and finish the site creation by clicking **Set up**. When the site is created, it displays under Sites as a protected site.

After a few seconds, the SDDC (JG-LAB-TEST) appears as a protected site in the console under the **Topology** window. See Figure 2-35.

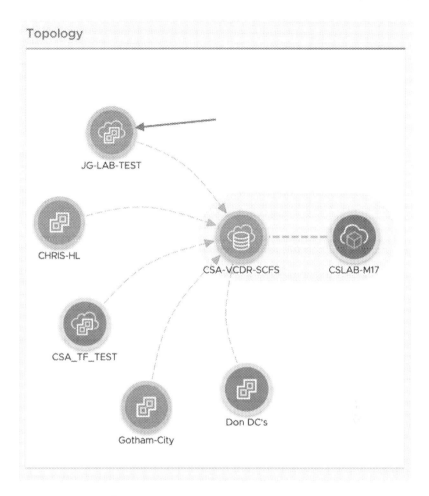

Figure 2-35. *Topology*

Once you have created the protected site, you can deploy the Cyber Recovery Connector.

Deploying the Cyber Recovery Connector

Once the site is configured, the next step is to deploy the Cyber Recovery Connector, which will enable the SaaS orchestrator to communicate with the protected Site vCenter. See Figure 2-36.

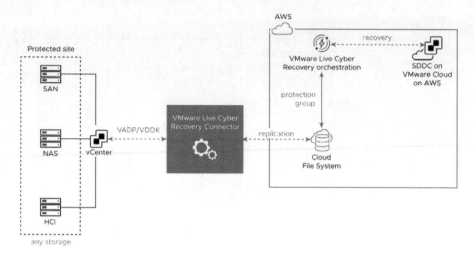

Figure 2-36. *VMware Live Cyber Recovery connector architecture*

To deploy the Cyber Recovery Connector virtual machine, make sure that the vSphere site where you intend to deploy it has the following available resources for the VM:

- CPU: 8 GHz (reserved)

- RAM: 12 GiB (reserved)

- Disk: 100 GiB vDisk

- Network connectivity between

    - the Connector and vCenter and ESXi hosts on the protected site

    - the Connector and VMware Cyber Recovery cloud resources

There are a couple of firewall ports that need to be configured to allow data replication traffic from the protected site datacenter to the cloud storage (SCFS); see Figure 2-37.

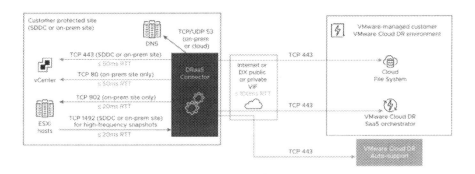

Figure 2-37. *Firewall ports to open from the VLCR connector*

At least one connector needs to be deploycd to create a protected site. The connector will need to be placed on a network configuration that can communicate with the local vCenter as well as the cloud components of VMware Cloud DR.

For on-premise sites, there is an OVA that gets installed into the target vCenter environment from the provided URL. This appliance VM provides the mechanism for coordinating the snapshot protection points and data replication to the cloud.

The process to deploy the connector is quite straightforward. Just click the **Deploy** button to get the details for the OVA. See Figure 2-38.

Figure 2-38. *Deploying the connector window*

In the Download connector dialog box, there is a list of steps that guide you in deploying the connector, as well as the URL to the connector OVA, with an option to download it locally to your system. See Figure 2-39.

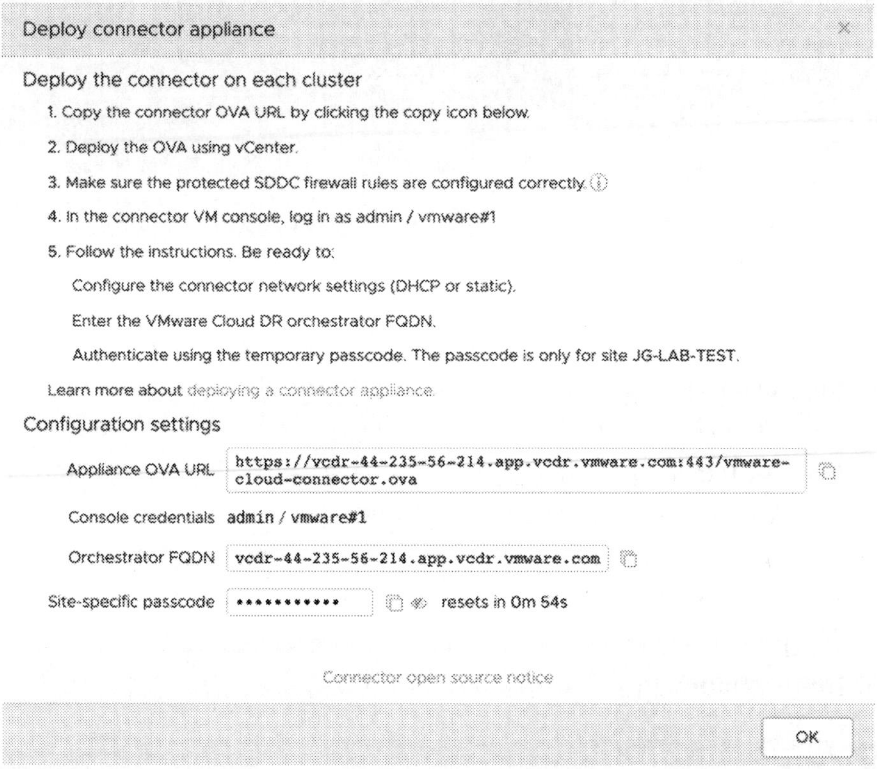

Deploy connector appliance   ✕

Deploy the connector on each cluster

    1. Copy the connector OVA URL by clicking the copy icon below.

    2. Deploy the OVA using vCenter.

    3. Make sure the protected SDDC firewall rules are configured correctly. ⓘ

    4. In the connector VM console, log in as admin / vmware#1

    5. Follow the instructions. Be ready to:

        Configure the connector network settings (DHCP or static).

        Enter the VMware Cloud DR orchestrator FQDN.

        Authenticate using the temporary passcode. The passcode is only for site JG-LAB-TEST.

Learn more about deploying a connector appliance.

Configuration settings

Appliance OVA URL	`https://vcdr-44-235-56-214.app.vcdr.vmware.com:443/vmware-cloud-connector.ova`
Console credentials	`admin / vmware#1`
Orchestrator FQDN	`vcdr-44-235-56-214.app.vcdr.vmware.com`
Site-specific passcode	••••••••••• resets in 0m 54s

Connector open source notice

OK

Figure 2-39. *Connector deployment – details for the OVA*

You can copy and paste the settings next to the Appliance OVA URL or Orchestrator FQDN.

Make a note of the **Console credentials**, which you need to log into the VM console: admin/vmware#1. Also copy (or write down) the **Orchestrator Fully Qualified Domain Name** (FQDN), which you need when you configure the connector in the VM console.

A few things you need to know:

- Do not name the connector VM using the same naming conventions you use to name VMs in your vSphere environment. Avoid giving the connector VM a name that might match the VM name pattern you use when you define protection groups.

- If you are deploying the connector to a VMware Cloud SDDC with more than one cluster, you must choose a cluster to deploy the connector VM on. Each cluster in your SDDC must have the connector VM deployed on it for the VMs running on the cluster to be added to protection groups and replicated to a cloud backup site.

- Do not use non-ASCII characters for the connector name label.

Copy the URL and download the OVA. After downloading the OVA by using the URL, you can upload the OVA to a content library in your vCenter and start the deployment of the OVA.

In vSphere, select any inventory object that is a valid parent object of a virtual machine, such as a data center, folder, cluster, resource pool, or host.

Right-click the object and select Actions ➤ **Deploy OVF Template**.

Select the OVA from the Content Library or past the OVA URL onto the URL field. See Figure 2-40.

Figure 2-40. *Deploying connector OVA*

Select a compute resource for the connector and give a name to the connector virtual machine. If this vSphere is a VMware Cloud on AWS SDDC with more than one cluster, choose a cluster to deploy the connector VM on. For an SDDC, each cluster you want to protect must have the Cyber Recovery Connector VM deployed on it. See Figure 2-41.

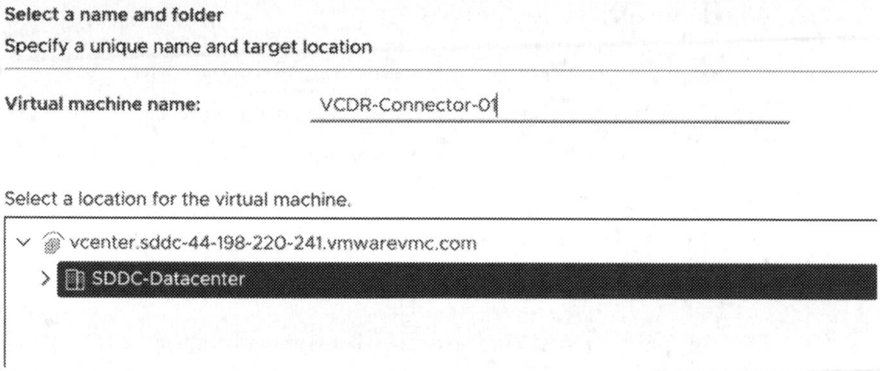

Select a name and folder
Specify a unique name and target location
Virtual machine name:
VCDR-Connector-01
Select a location for the virtual machine.
vcenter.sddc-44-198-220-241.vmwarevmc.com
SDDC-Datacenter

Figure 2-41. *Deploying connector OVA – folder selection*

Pick a resource pool (for a VMware Cloud on AWS SDDC, the only resource pool available is the Compute-Resource Pool). See Figure 2-42.

SDDC-Datacenter
Cluster-1
10.10.10.68
Compute-ResourcePool
Mgmt-ResourcePool
10.10.11.217

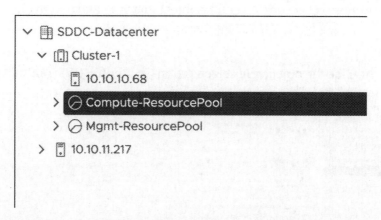

Figure 2-42. *Deploying connector OVA – resource pool selection*

Review the details for your connector deployment and then click Next to select storage for the connector VM. In a VMware Cloud on AWS SDDC, the storage datastore can only be the WorkloadDatastore, as shown in Figure 2-43.

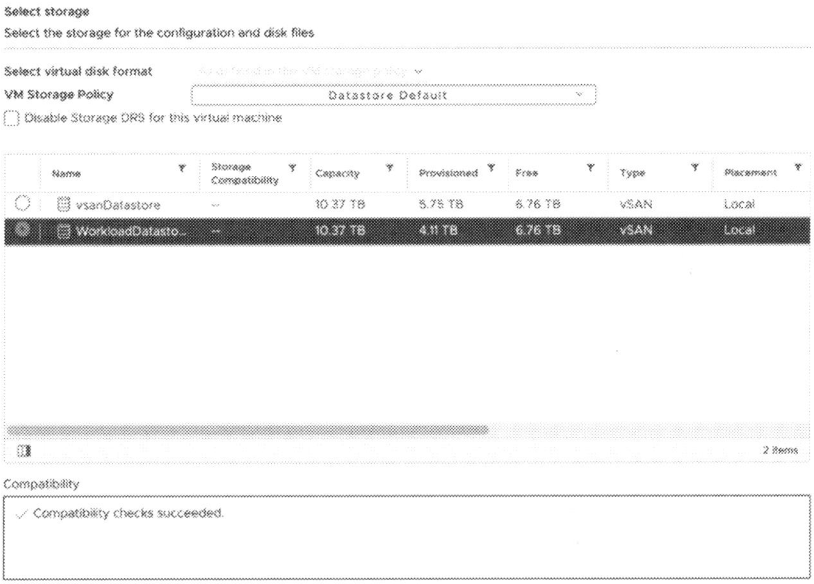

Figure 2-43. *Deploying connector OVA – datastore selection*

Select the network to use for the connector and then click Next to review the deployment detail. In a VMware Cloud on AWS, you can choose the default compute segment (sddc-cgw-network-1). See Figure 2-44.

Figure 2-44. *Deploying connector OVA – network selection*

You will be presented with the final page of the wizard where you can click Finish to launch the deployment.

After a few seconds, the Connector Virtual Machine appears in the inventory.

Power on the connector VM and log in to complete the configuration setup such as network and site details. See Figure 2-45.

Figure 2-45. *Connector description under vCenter*

Once the connector virtual machine has been powered on, you must finish the configuration including the networking settings. The connector can either be configured via the vSphere Web Console or via SSH if a DHCP IP address is used.

When using the web console from vCenter, connect with the credential presented in the deploy connector appliance window: `admin/vmware#1`. See Figure 2-46.

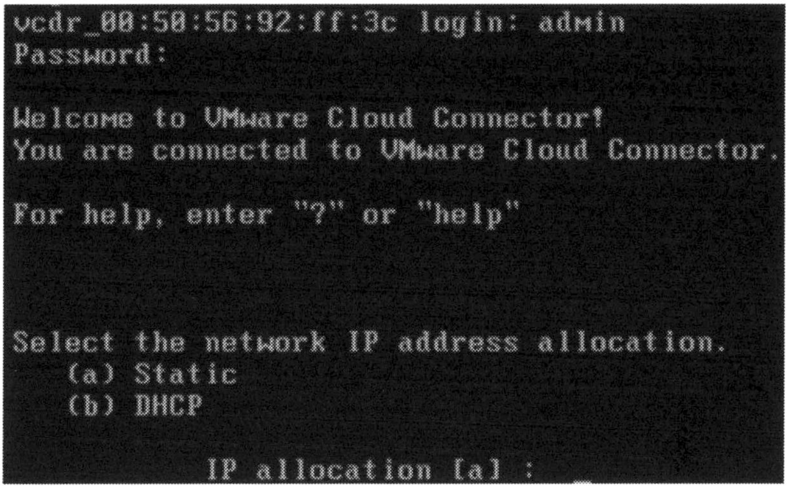

```
vcdr_00:50:56:92:ff:3c login: admin
Password:

Welcome to VMware Cloud Connector!
You are connected to VMware Cloud Connector.

For help, enter "?" or "help"



Select the network IP address allocation.
    (a) Static
    (b) DHCP

            IP allocation [a] :  _
```

Figure 2-46. *Connector configuration – Welcome console*

Type a to start Static IP allocation and enter a new IP address and subnet mask plus a DNS IP address (e.g., Google DNS), as shown in Figure 2-47.

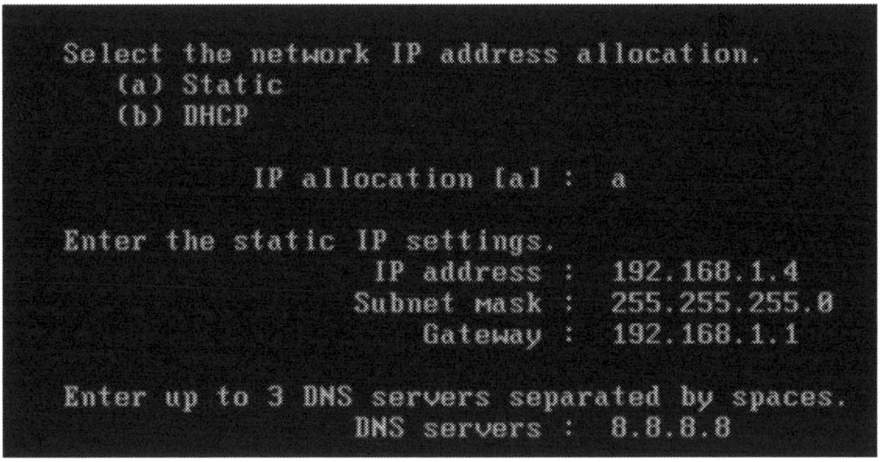

```
Select the network IP address allocation.
    (a) Static
    (b) DHCP

            IP allocation [a] :   a

Enter the static IP settings.
                IP address :   192.168.1.4
                Subnet mask :   255.255.255.0
                Gateway :   192.168.1.1

Enter up to 3 DNS servers separated by spaces.
                DNS servers :   8.8.8.8
```

Figure 2-47. *Connector networking configuration*

The next step is to enter the Cloud Orchestrator FQDN. See Figure 2-48.

Figure 2-48. *Connector configuration – Cloud DR orchestrator FQDN*

And to achieve the configuration add the site specific pass-code and the site label (you can keep the same name as the VM).

After a few seconds, if all is good, you will receive a Success message to inform you that the setup is achieved, as shown in Figure 2-49.

Figure 2-49. *Connector configuration – success message*

Once the connector is installed and configured, it must be registered with the vCenter that contains the VMs to be protected.

Registering vCenter

Now you need to register the vCenter to your protected site. This step is only needed if it is an on-premises environment. If the protected site is a VMware Cloud on AWS SDDC, the vCenter will be automatically registered for you and you will not have to perform this step.

1. Click Register vCenter.

2. Enter the vCenter Server IP address.

3. Enter the vCenter administrator username and
    password.

4. Click Register.

Once registered, the vCenter will appear in the vCenter section of the
protected site.

The protected site is now defined and ready to use to build the DR
strategy by creating Protection Groups and DR Plans.

2.2.5 Implementing a DR Strategy

Once Live Cyber Recovery has been procured and ready to deploy, your
DR administrators can follow a similar set of tasks to get your organization
ready for failover to the cloud in short order.

Implementing your DR strategy with Live Cyber Recovery is a five-step
process:

Step 1 – Planification

- Determine the VMs to be protected by VMware Live
  Cyber Recovery and organize them into preliminary
  application DR sets for protection policy assignment
  and DR plans step(s) processing.

- Align available SLAs to protection policies (e.g., 4
  hours, 15 minutes, or daily, weekly, monthly) and
  initial retention objectives to be applied after the initial
  snapshot.

- Define and document the protected site organization
  of compute resources, folders, networks, and tags
  that may be used to identify and place VMs in the
  Recovery SDDC.

Step 2 – Define the policies

- Construct the protected site(s) that contain the target VMs.

- Construct a test protection group for a small sample VM set for each protected site to verify basic site to site operations.

- Construct initial protection group policies for the VMs defined in the application DR sets in Step 1 (set inactive for this phase).

- Take manual snapshots of protection groups. Use relative prioritization and/or data set size to optimize initial transfer readiness.

Step 3 – Configure the strategy and plans

- Deploy the VMware Cloud SDDC test site. Use a one-host (temporary) footprint to minimize costs and familiarize yourself with the process.

- Modify the Recovery SDDC to the desired configuration to align with protected site(s). This includes resource groups, folders, networks, tags, and "test bubbles" setup.

- Define DR plans using the application organization details from Step 1.

Step 4 – Test the failover and DR strategy

- Begin DR plan failover testing using the NFS live mount datastore for initial steps alignment.

- Run a DR plan test with full SDDC migration (Storage vMotion) to understand operational results.

- Adjust DR plans based on any performance or sizing findings in the testing processes.

Step 5 – Operate the plans

- Review reports for compliance and plan details.

- Review runbooks for test runs from Step 4.

- Monitor progress of protected site protection and compliance checking.

- Document and remove the "test" SDDC.

Protecting Virtual Machines with Protection Groups

Protection Groups are a very important object when setting up the DR plan and strategy. They are a way of grouping virtual machines that will be recovered together.

A Protection Group contains virtual machines whose data will be replicated by the VMware Live Cyber Recovery connector to the SCFS following the same protection policy.

The protection policy defines the frequency when snapshots are taken and how long the recovery point is retained in the cloud-based SCFS.

In many cases, a Protection Group will consist of the virtual machines that support a service or application such as email or an accounting system. For example, an application might consist of a two-server database cluster, three application servers, and four web servers. In most cases, it would not be beneficial to failover part of this application, so all virtual machines would be included in a single Protection Group.

Creating a Protection Group for each application or service has the benefit of selective testing.

In the examples shown here, there are three separate Protection Groups: Web App, Email, and SharePoint. See Figure 2-50.

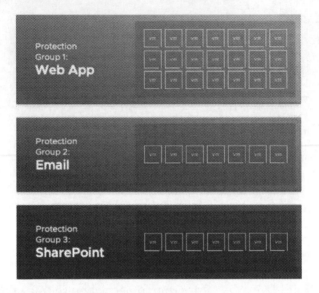

Figure 2-50. *Example of Protection Groups*

Having a Protection Group for each application enables non-disruptive, low risk testing of individual applications, allowing application owners to non-disruptively test disaster recovery plans as needed.

The default snapshot method uses "VMware vSphere Storage APIs – Data Protection" to access the changed blocks for each snapshot allows the VMs to reside on any supported datastore.

You can create multiple groups of VMs through multiple protection groups.

A Protection Group consists of the following components:

- Site selection (on-premises or SDDC vCenter)

- Members (VMs)

- Policies for snapshots (schedule, retention)

- Cloud backup site (SCFS)

To create a Protection Group, give it a name, select the protected site, and the vCenter from which the VMs will be selected.

- Cloud backup is automatically selected.

It will tell if **high frequency snapshots** (HFSs) are supported.

- HFS allows snapshots every **30 minutes**.

- **SDDC version > 1.16**

- **VMs with snapshots are excluded.**

You can do a **host compatibility check** for **HFS**.

Quiescing of the OS guest is possible through VSS support for **OS** only and **VADP** snapshots (this does not work with HFS, however). See Figure 2-51.

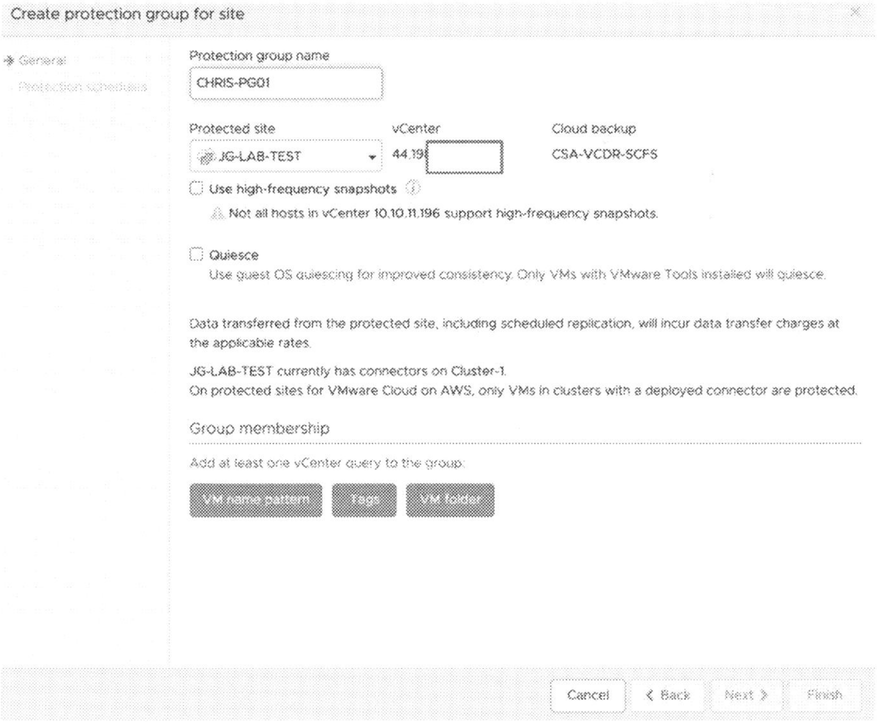

Figure 2-51. Protection Group settings

To select the list of VMs, you must create one vCenter query that defines the Protection Group's dynamic membership.

A vCenter query is defined using

- **VM name pattern**: A name pattern is a regex entry that supports wildcard and exclusion.

- **VM folder**: A folder where my VMs run

- **VM tags**: vSphere tags for quickly identifying the logical membership of VMs. See Figure 2-52.

Figure 2-52. *Virtual machine selection – VM name pattern*

VM pattern tips

- , to separate patterns

- * matches zero or more characters

- ? matches exactly one character

- If there are multiple patterns, they are separated by or.

You can also create **tags**. When you create a new tag, you first need to create a category.

Click **Preview VMs**. It will list the VM that is going to be selected in the next snapshot. Anytime you add a new VM with the corresponding tag, it will automatically be added to the Protection Group. See Figure 2-53.

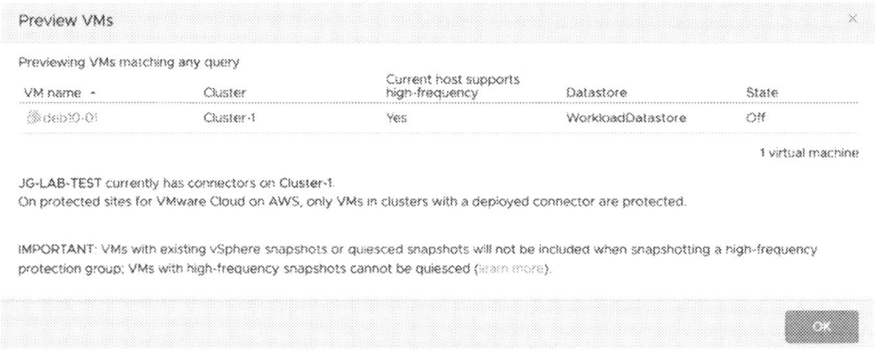

Figure 2-53. *VM preview in Protection Groups*

You can also just pick VMs from **folders**. VMs in subfolders are not added automatically.

You can't have one Protection Group with tags and folders, for example.

NB   Virtual machines can belong to more than one protection group.

Setting up a protection policy: Once you have your VM selected, the next step is to define a backup policy with specific snapshot/replication schedule and retention time.

The snapshot schedule will define how frequently you want to take snapshots of the VMs defined in the group. You also define how long you want to retain those snapshots on the SCFS by selecting the right retention time.

Establishing a good protection strategy implies the following:

1. Determining what data must be backed up.

2. Understanding how often data must be backed up.

3. Testing and monitoring your backup system.

The minimum replication schedule that you can set up (best RPO possible) is 15 minutes.

Define how long you want to keep the replication points in the cloud.

NB   The more time you replicate, the more you keep it in the cloud, the more capacity you need on the cloud site for recovery purposes.

A comprehensive replication strategy with short term and relatively longer term for ransomware use case or other is as shown in Figure 2-54 (it has to be adapted with each workload's needs based on their criticality).

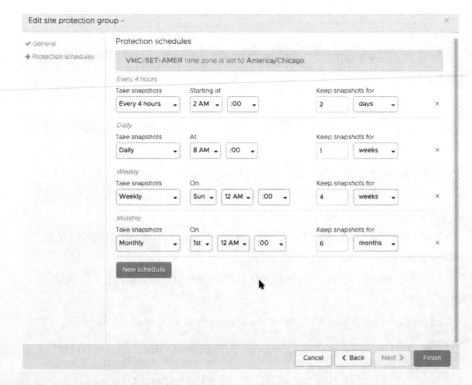

Figure 2-54. *Setting up a protection schedule*

Best practices for the policy:

- Use the minimal RTO with a short retention time.

- A daily backup with a retention of one week to cover short-term recovery needs.

- Weekly and monthly backup with longer retention to cover compliance needs.

- The retention period of existing snapshots is not affected if you change to a longer or shorter retention date in the settings. It applies only to new snapshots.

Important   Research indicates most victims of ransomware don't discover that they have been compromised until an average of 3-6 months after the initial infection, so choose the retention period accordingly.

Once you have defined your replication strategy and protection schedule for your group of virtual machines, the policy runs automatically based on the schedule and the snapshots/replicas start populating in the protection group.

Each point-in-time snapshot recovery point is stored in the SCFS offsite, on cloud efficient storage. Each recovery point is an immutable snapshot independent of the others in the collection. The delta-changed blocks transmitted from the connector are transformed into a synthetic full representation of the VMs in the Protection Group.

The recovery points are listed in the detailed view for the Protection Group.

You can click on any snapshots and see the VMs inside any of them. See Figure 2-55.

CHRIS-PG01

Group details	Membership	Schedule
Snapshots 3	VM name pattern "deb"	*Every 4 hours:* snapshot every four hours starting at 12:00 AM. Retain for 2 days
Schedule Active		*Daily:* snapshot every day at 12:00 AM. Retain for 1 week
Health OK		*Weekly:* snapshot every week on Sun at 12:00 AM. Retain for 4 weeks
Site JG-LAB-TEST		*Monthly:* snapshot every month on the 1st at 12:00 AM. Retain for 12 months
Type High-frequency		Site time zone: New York, America

Snapshots   Delete

Times are shown in time zone Paris, Europe. JG-LAB-TEST is using New York, America (03:32 am).

Name	Taken timestamp	Includes	Total size	Expiration
CHRIS-PG01 - Every 4 hours Daily - 2025-12-17T08:00 UTC	Dec-17 06:00 am (4h ago)	1 VM	1.5 GiB	Dec-24 06:00 am (in 7d)
CHRIS-PG01 - Every 4 hours - 2025-12-17T02:00 UTC	Dec-17 02:00 am (8h ago)	1 VM	1.5 GiB	Dec-19 02:00 am (in 2d)
CHRIS-PG01 - Every 4 hours - 2025-12-16T22:00 UTC	Dec-16 10:01 pm (12h ago)	1 VM	1.5 GiB	Dec-18 10:01 pm (in 2d)

Figure 2-55. *Point-in-time snapshots inside the Protection Group*

And you have the option to restore any image of a virtual machine back to on-premises. This is an image-level backup so this will overwrite the virtual machine on-premises. In consequence, the VM must be **powered down** before doing so.

Deploying the Recovery Sites

VMware Live Cyber Recovery propose two options to spin up a recovery SDDC to bring up the virtual machines in case of a failover scenario for both disaster and ransomware recovery:

- **On-demand**: Also known as "just in time" deployment. With this option, you get the required storage for snapshots on the SCFS and when you want to execute tests or recover, an SDDC is spun up and you can recover your workloads in a matter of minutes.

- **Pilot Light**: You have a small subset (at least a two-node cluster) of VMware Cloud on AWS SDDC that is ready to go and ready to take over the VMs in case of a DR with the lowest RTO. You can do all your testing in it and get all your reports for compliance whenever you like. Since the SDDC is already deployed, in case of a DR event, you don't have to wait for an SDDC to be spun up; you can get right to it and get the virtual machines back.

VMware Live Cyber Recovery supports recovery SDDCs using i3, i3en, and i4i hosts.

There are two ways to attach a recovery SDDC to a VMware Live Cyber Recovery deployment:

- Deploy a recovery SDDC from the web UI.

- Attach an existing SDDC that has been deployed earlier.

When deploying a brand new SDDC in VMware Cloud AWS, you must provide the following information:

- SDDC name

- Type of hosts

- Number of hosts (A single host can be deployed but only for testing purposes. It's always possible to scale it up and add additional hosts in it. If you want a production SDDC, it has to be a two-node cluster at minimum.)

- Region and zone (make sure it is in the same AZ as the SCFS)

- Management subnet: Minimum CIDR sizes are /23 for up to 27 hosts, /20 for up to 251 hosts, and /16 for up to 4091 hosts

- Compute subnet: It can't overlap with existing networks on-premises.

- Proxy subnet: A /26 subnet is needed by the solution and it has to be distinct from the management subnet.

NB   VMware Live Cyber Recovery does not currently support stretched clusters for a recovery SDDC.

Once the SDDC is created and linked to the SCFS, you can access its settings from the web UI of VMware Live Cyber Recovery and adjust them. You can, for instance, customize the networking configuration from here by adding network segments and firewall rules.

To finalize the DR strategy once you have deployed the recovery SDDC, you can create a **DR Plan** and test it.

Disaster Recovery Plans

The DR strategy is enforced through the concept of a DR Plan. Let's look a bit more closely at the details and structure of a DR plan.

It basically defines what is going to fail over, where it's going to go in the cloud, how it's going to come in online, and in what order.

A DR plan is where you define the different parameters that sustain the strategy including defining the protected resources, the orchestration order of the recovery process, and several additional options when the failover executes like changing the IP addresses or executing scripts.

The recovery of workloads and applications is managed and controlled by the Recovery Plan that specifies the order in which virtual machines can be restored, the required resource pools, the storage, and the network they can access through the concept of resource mappings.

VMware Live Cyber Recovery can maintain multiple plans of different types, and the plans can be in various stages of execution at any given time, even concurrently.

Protection Groups are the basis for defining the scope of a DR Plan. Protection Groups identify the virtual machines that are to be handled by the failover orchestration.

A DR Plan can contain more than one Protection Group and a Protection Group can appear in more than one DR Plan.

In the examples in Figure 2-56, you see three separate DR plans, based on the previous Protection Groups: Web App, Email, SharePoint (one for the Web App, one for the SharePoint applications, and one that can be used to failover all the applications).

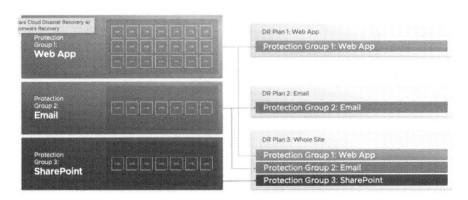

Figure 2-56. *Example of DR Plans*

You can also add recovery steps for the orchestration on how you want the VMs to come up in what order and what customization you want to do per virtual machines. You can recover DB first, then application servers, and front-end servers in the third step, for instance.

Examples of these special actions are as follows:

- Wait for user input

- Timed delay so that something can happen in the environment

- Run a script on the script virtual machine

Each of the steps also has pre and post actions available as a virtual machine is brought into inventory and powered on and adjusted. You can have plans to take steps before and after this recovery action.

With these plan construction capabilities, you can have a simple recovery sequence of events or a very robust and detailed set of actions in the DR Plan specifications. See Figure 2-57.

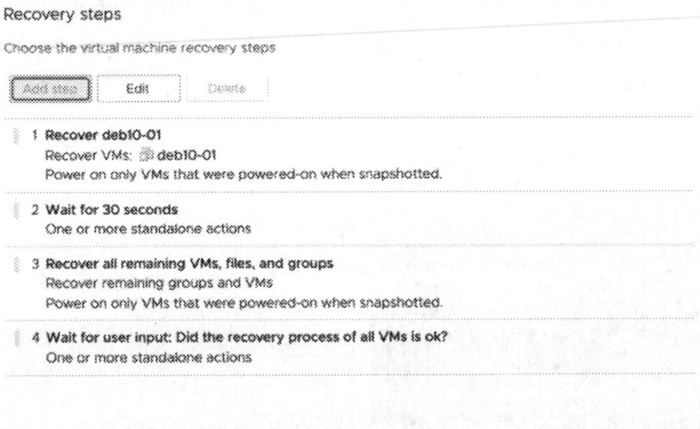

Figure 2-57. *Recovery steps in DR Plans*

A continuous compliance check against the DR Plans is automatically run every 30 minutes to make sure the plan will work as designed when needed.

Every plan has the option of doing a test failover or an actual failover. The difference between a failover and a test is that a failback will be required to post a failover but in a test you just bring a copy of your VM in the cloud and a failback is not needed because you don't want to overwrite the existing VMs on premise.

During a failover and test you take the recovery point you want to recover from, which could be minutes, months, or even many years old. Once selected, they are going to be instantly powered on from the scale-out cloud file system that is already live mounted directly to the SDDC, resulting in low RTO[6].

The following operations are allowed under the DR Plan section:

- **Configuring DR Plans**: Defining where you want your protected data moved to when the plan runs

- **Viewing DR Plans**: Shows the currently defined plans along with plan summary information: the current status, protected and recovery sites, and the last run compliance check results

- **Activating DR Plans**: A plan can either be in an active or deactivated state.

Creating a DR Plan

Follow these steps to configure a DR Plan:

1. To create a DR Plan, click **Create plan** from the DR plans menu, as shown in Figure 2-58.

---

[6] The targeted amount of time a business process should be restored after a disaster or disruption in order to avoid unacceptable consequences associated with a break in business continuity

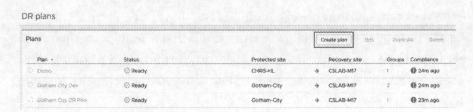

Figure 2-58. *DR Plan creation*

2. Give the plan a name and choose the recovery site
for the failover option. You can either choose an
existing Recovery SDDC or that a **Recovery SDDC is
deployed** when a DR event occurs. See Figure 2-59.

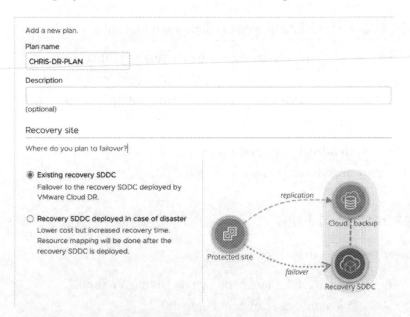

Figure 2-59. *Creating a DR Plan – recovery site*

3. Choose the **protected site** (in case you have more
than one, choose the site where the Protection
Group is created). See Figure 2-60.

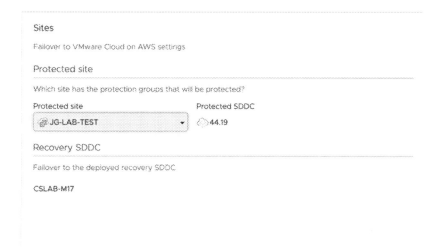

Figure 2-60. *Creating a DR Plan – protected site (SDDC example)*

4. Grab the **Protection Group** that would be failed
    over when this DR plan is executed. Take one
    you have defined earlier. You can select multiple
    Protection Groups. See Figure 2-61.

    •   Per application Protection Groups are a good
        practice; a DR Plan can use all of them for a
        datacenter-wide DR.

Figure 2-61. *Creating a DR Plan – Protection Group*

- The next steps are to map the different resources (datastores, folders, resource pools, virtual networks) from the protected to the recovery site.

- It's very important to map differences between the sites for smooth recovery, ensuring that vSphere configurations and parameters are mapped consistently between sites.

Folders Mapping

5. Map the protected site workload folders to the corresponding one in the recovery SDDC. In Figure 2-62, I mapped the "my Workloads" folders on both sites. When you select folders, it shows in blue the one where VMs are standing.

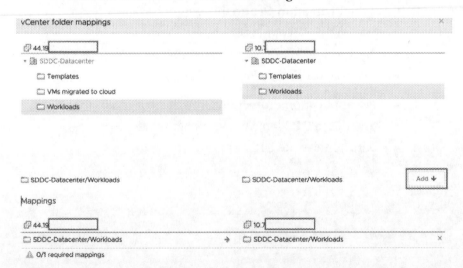

Figure 2-62. *Folders mappings in the DR Plan*

Compute Resource Pools Mapping

6. Keep the same mapping for the resource pools
   (this requires creating the right resource pools on
   the recovery SDDC prior to starting the DR plan
   creation). See Figure 2-63.

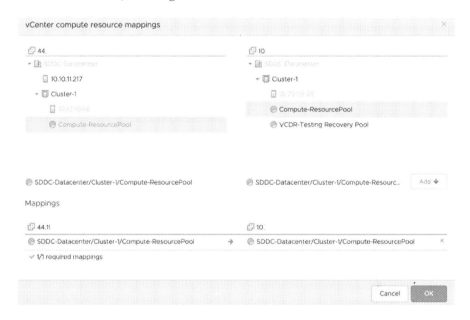

Figure 2-63. *Creating a DR Plan – resource pools mapping*

Network Mapping

7. Next is the subnet mappings that require again to
   anticipate the creation of the equivalent subnets in
   the Recovery SDDC. See Figure 2-64.

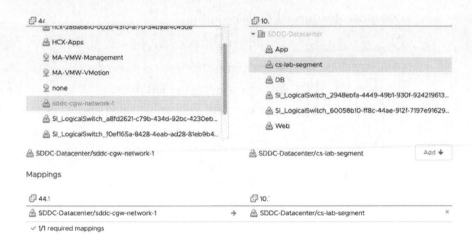

Figure 2-64. *DR plan creation – network mappings*

Keep in mind that test and failover **mappings** can
be different by unselecting the ***Same for test and
failover*** button. Maybe you want to use a different
subnet for testing (for instance an isolated one). See
Figure 2-65.

Figure 2-65. *Test mapping options*

8. The next thing is the **IP address mapping rules.**
    These rules change the range of IPs, subnet masks,
    and DNS settings at failover time. It does that by
    interacting with the *VM Tools* in the VM while it's
    running. See Figure 2-66.

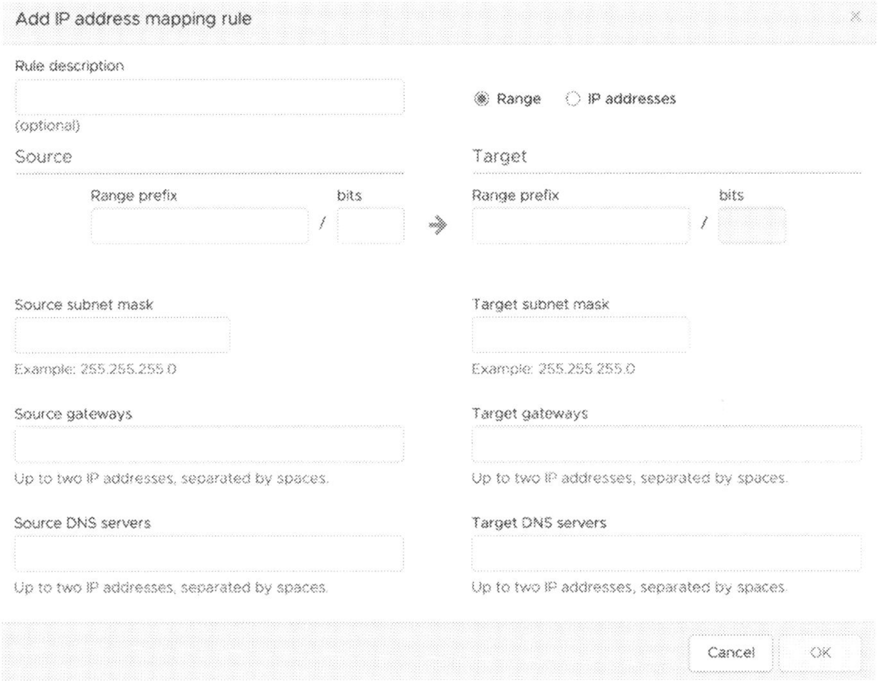

Add IP address mapping rule   ✕

Rule description

[   ]   ⦿ Range   ○ IP addresses
(optional)

Source   Target

       Range prefix   bits   Range prefix   bits

       [   ] / [   ]   ⇒   [   ] / [   ]

Source subnet mask   Target subnet mask

[   ]   [   ]

Example: 255.255.255.0   Example: 255.255.255.0

Source gateways   Target gateways

[   ]   [   ]

Up to two IP addresses, separated by spaces. Up to two IP addresses, separated by spaces.

Source DNS servers   Target DNS servers

[   ]   [   ]

Up to two IP addresses, separated by spaces. Up to two IP addresses, separated by spaces.

                                                    Cancel   OK

Figure 2-66. DR plan creation – IP address mappings

You can change the IP/mask/default GW/DNS
addresses on a range basis or an individual IP
addresses basis.

Script VM

9. Next is the ability to execute a script of any language
    for both **Windows (PowerShell)** and **Linux
    (Python)** machine types from a script host. The
    script can be executed at a specified time from this
    script VM. It can be any script of any language. You
    just need to designate a Windows or Linux virtual
    machine as a script host and it will call the script
    with parameters of your choice.

The **script VM** needs to be running in the
Recovery SDDC and available from the vCenter
of the recovery SDDC. You call the script from the
VM with any parameters you want to be running
during the failover sequence. See Figure 2-67.

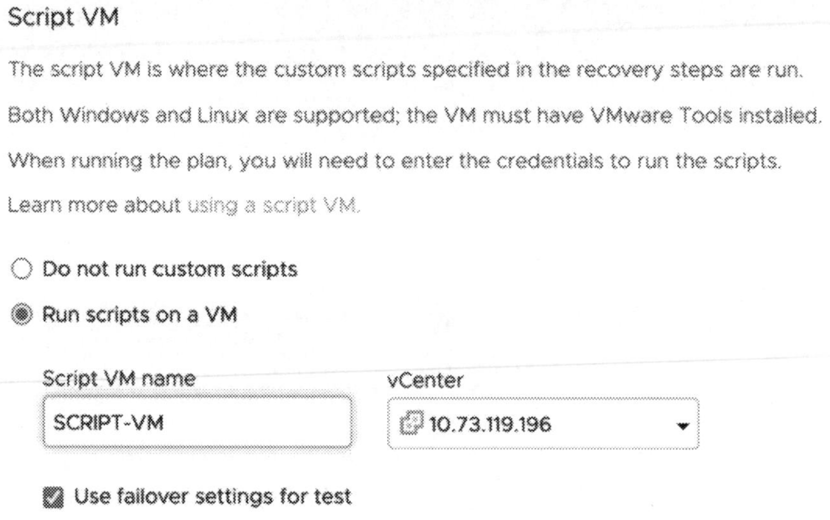

Script VM

The script VM is where the custom scripts specified in the recovery steps are run.

Both Windows and Linux are supported; the VM must have VMware Tools installed.

When running the plan, you will need to enter the credentials to run the scripts.

Learn more about using a script VM.

○ Do not run custom scripts

◉ Run scripts on a VM

Script VM name   vCenter

| SCRIPT-VM | | 🖥 10.73.119.196   ▾ |

☑ Use failover settings for test

Figure 2-67. *Script VM configuration in the DR Plan*

NB   You cannot use a script VM during ransomware recovery.

---

10.   Enter the name of the VM on which the script is
going to run and choose a location to save the
custom scripts.

Recovery Steps

11.   To finish, the recovery steps specify the order in
which you want your VMs to be recovered. There are
different options.

a. Choose a step that can be executed for either whole protection groups or an individual VM under the Protection Group.

b. Select the Power action for recovered VMs.

12. Select pre-recover or post-recover actions from the drop-down menu, which can run scripts that were saved under step 4 above. See Figure 2-68.

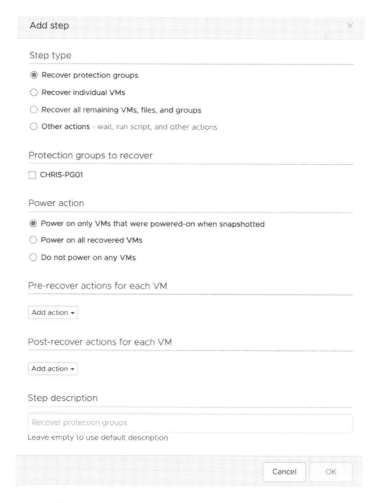

Figure 2-68. *Adding recovery steps in a DR Plan*

Adding recovery steps in a Recovery Plan can help specify what actions the plan should take during a failover or failback. You can add recovery steps for the orchestration on how you want the VMs to come up in what order and what customization you want to do per VM. For example, you can recover the DB first, then application servers, and front-end servers in the third step. You can also select individual VMs.

There are a couple of other actions you can launch:

- You can choose the order of the recovery.

- You can run a script that is not related to the VMs recovered.

- You also have the option to configure how you want the running plan to handle errors during failover or failback operations.

- You can wait for a user input before finishing a task. There is a custom dialog box that pops up in the UI in this case.

- You can wait for a fixed amount of time to pause the execution of the plan. See Figure 2-69.

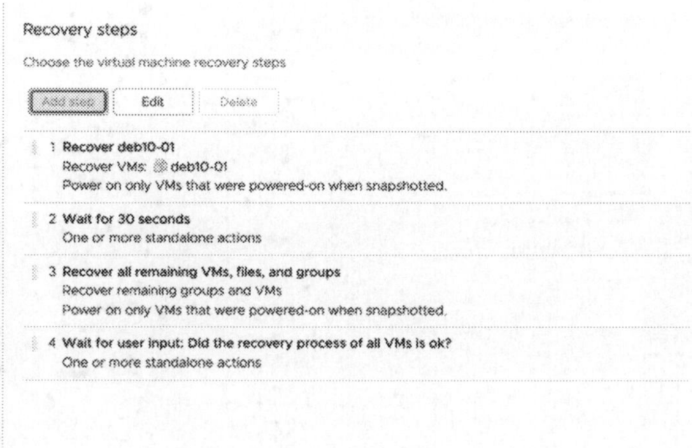

Recovery steps

Choose the virtual machine recovery steps

[Add step] [Edit] [Delete]

1 **Recover deb10-01**
   Recover VMs: deb10-01
   Power on only VMs that were powered-on when snapshotted.

2 **Wait for 30 seconds**
   One or more standalone actions

3 **Recover all remaining VMs, files, and groups**
   Recover remaining groups and VMs
   Power on only VMs that were powered-on when snapshotted.

4 **Wait for user input: Did the recovery process of all VMs is ok?**
   One or more standalone actions

Figure 2-69. *Recovery steps*

It's possible to drag and drop the tasks and move them to a different position.

- It's possible to recover a single VM or a group of VMs.

- The **Recover all remaining VMs, files, and groups** step must be the last recovery step.

- You can also define an action before or after powering up the VMs during a failover or failback. Add the absolute path to the script. Add **custom parameters** when you go to execute that script. By default, it includes a few parameters. Scc Figure 2-70.

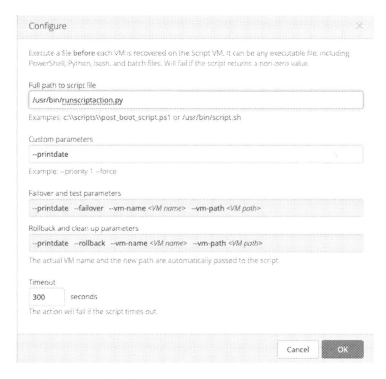

Figure 2-70. *Example of a script parameter*

- Select the different options under the recovery steps.

  a. Choose a step that can be executed for either whole Protection Groups or an individual VM under the Protection Group.

  b. Select the power action for recovered VMs. A recovery step requires one of the three power actions:

      i.   Power-on only VMs that were powered-on when the snapshot was taken.

      ii. Power-on all recovered VMs.

      iii. Do not power on VMs.

  c. Select pre-recover or post-recover actions from the drop-down menu, which can run scripts saved under step 4 above.

2.3 Operational Aspects of VMware LCR

Let's go over how to execute the DR Plans and to monitor the activities related to executing the failover testing or the actual failover and failback in case of a disaster.

2.3.1 Managing DR Plan

Activating a Plan

A disaster recovery plan can be in either an active or deactivated state.

When in active state, you can run and execute failover and failback operations. Every newly created plan will be activated. When you execute a failover or failback successfully, a DR plan will be deactivated. You can reactivate it at any time by clicking **Activate plan**.

NB   When a DR plan is deactivated, there is no compliance check against it.

The Active plan state is indicated in the Status column of the Recovery Plan list. Depending on whether the test site is configured, an active plan can have either Ready or Ready (not testable) status. See Figure 2-71.

Figure 2-71.   *DR Plan status*

Executing a Failover

Before executing a DR Plan, you must have done the following:

- Defined a protected site where at least one connector is deployed

- Created the protection groups with the VMs to protect and with scheduled snapshots

- Have the target recovery SDDC ready with the equivalent tags and networking configuration (prepare the segments prior to the creation of the DR plan to be able to do the network mappings)

Let's assume that you have all the components in place and setup tasks accomplished and want to declare that you are "ready for DR." What does that mean?

Failover readiness is the confidence that you can fail over application workloads from your on-premise data center to VMware Cloud on AWS.

The first step is to make sure you have an SDDC deployed. This SDDC can be a just in time, it can be a Pilot Light, or it can be a fully provisioned cloud site.

Every plan has the option of doing a *test failover* or an actual *failover*. You can execute a recovery plan for ransom recovery as well (see the next chapter).

Testing the plan: With an SDDC to connect to, it is possible to test the DR plan frequently to familiarize yourself with the process and make sure it's working well. Testing can be non-disruptive to the production workloads as DR plan mappings, for example, for networking or IP changes allow for failover and testing pairings enabling isolation during testing actions. Nothing is affected in the source on-premises environment during a plan testing action. During functional testing runs, you can choose to leave workloads running on the live mount datastore, saving test cycle time in many cases.

For more performance related testing, the workloads can be migrated fully into the SDDC, as they would during an actual failover event, to ensure all SLAs are being met.

Running the plan: In the event of an actual failover, the DR Plan starts the virtual machines on the live mount datastore so you can get back into operations sooner and then migrates the VM storage to the SDDC in the background if needed. It is important to note that during test runs, cloud-based data changes are not captured when the test is completed and cleaned up. During an actual failover, there are two scenario for the recovery steps execution that generates two types of workflows:

- **Planned**: This creates a workflow of operations based on the recovery steps defined in the DR plan.

- **Unplanned**: In this case, the workflow is shorter and no VMs are powered off on the source site and there is no final replication of data.

During a failover or a failover test, you take the recovery point you want to recover from. You can choose the recovery point that you want for your failover or your test. This could be the last good replication from on premises to the cloud file system or something older. It could be anything that your protection group retention SLAs have established. It could be hours, days, weeks, or even months old.

You can use this recovery point for a near term failover or possibly for recovery from something that struck your environment days or weeks ago such as ransomware and you're just now discovering it.

When you execute a failover or do a test failover, you have the option to run failed-over VMs directly from the cloud file system or to have them fully migrated to the VSAN datastore inside the SDDC

Let's see in more detail each option for the VM storage:

- **Full storage migration to the SDDC**: In this case, you map the file system over NFS, and in the background, there is a storage vMotion onto the vSAN storage within the SDDC. The RTO increases when you use this option as data must be moved to the VSAN datastore. Indeed, the plan cannot be finished and committed until the operations are finished.

- **Leave VMs and files in the SCFS (backed by S3 storage and EC2 front-end caching)**: This offers a faster failover time and a better RTO as VMs run directly from the cloud filesystem. However, the SCFS is not going to be as performant as all flash vSAN. It's capped at 500MB of throughput and 50K IOPS. Indeed, SCFS is backed by S3 storage, and it is known to be cheap and highly durable but it's not known to be highly performant. If you need greater performance for a highly transactional database, you need to use vSAN. See Figure 2-72.

Figure 2-72. *Configure VM storage for failover*

It's a best practice to separate the VMs into different protection groups and recovery plans based on their storage performance needs as you won't be able to choose between the two options VM by VM when running a plan.

NB   If you first chose to run VMs from the cloud file system, you can decide later to migrate them to the VSAN datastore (WorkloadDatastore).

When a DR Plan has finished executing and all of the steps in the running plan have completed, you must explicitly commit a failover or rollback and acknowledge a failback plan in order for the plan to return to a ready state.

The procedure to run a failover is as follow:

- Select Recovery Plans and select the plan you
  want to run.

- Click the DR Failover button.

- Choose the snapshot state to be used to run the test
  recovery from the Snapshots page. See Figure 2-73.

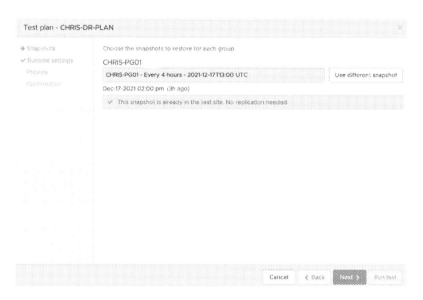

Figure 2-73. *Grabbing a snapshot during a failover execution*

By default, the system proposes the latest snapshot. You can choose
a different protection group snapshot if you prefer to recover from a later
time. See Figure 2-74.

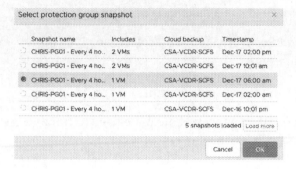

Figure 2-74. *Selecting a different protection group snapshot for failover*

- In the Runtime settings page, under Error handling you can select between the following two options:

    - **Ignore all errors**. The runtime default is to ignore all errors.

    - **Stop on every error**: Choose this option if you are running this plan as a test failover. See Figure 2-75.

Figure 2-75. *Error handling during a failover*

- Select the storage options.

- Click **Next**.

- In the Preview Page, you can view all the steps that are going to be taken, as shown in Figure 2-76.

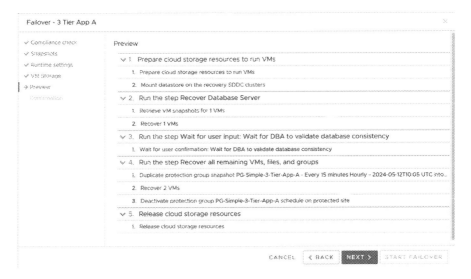

Figure 2-76. *Execution of a plan failover – preview of tasks*

- Click **Next**.

- Confirm that you want to execute the plan by entering FAILOVER in all upper case letters in the confirmation text box. See Figure 2-77.

Figure 2-77. Confirming failover

When it begins running, the plan moves into the failover state. You can observe the running plan's progress from the plan's detail page.

If you choose to do a full storage migration, you can also observe the storage VMotion from the Staging datastore to the SDDC datastore following VM recovery.

While a plan runs, you can perform the following operations:

- Cancel/Cancel and rollback

- Wait for user input

- Terminate

Failover Testing

After creating a Recovery Plan, it is important to regularly test the it to verify it works as expected. VMware Live Cyber Recovery features a non-disruptive testing mechanism to facilitate testing at any time. It is common for an organization to test a Recovery Plan multiple times after creation to resolve any issues encountered the first time it was tested.

A test failover runs in the context of its own test failover environment, specified by the DR plan's test mapping rules. The results of the test failover do not permanently affect a target failover destination.

You can choose the snapshot state to be used to run the test recovery. A test failover stops on the first failure by default. You can override all other default behavior using custom options.

The difference between a failover and a test is that a failback will be required post a failover while in a test you are just bringing a copy of your VM in the cloud and a failback is not needed because you don't want or need to overwrite the existing VMs on premise.

Failback is required after a failover, meaning once you are running in the cloud, you want to bring the data back to on-premises once the event is over. When you are doing a test, it is one way.

The first thing you're asked during a failover test is which snapshot you want to go to. The program defaults to the latest snapshot. If you click using different, you can grab any of them.

During a **test failover** there are also two options for the data:

- **Full storage migration to the SDDC**: You map the FS over NFS and in the background you store vMotion onto the vSAN storage within the SDDC.

- **Leave VMs and files in the SCFS**: In Step 1, you prepare the NFS mount. It takes the system a few minutes to mount and verify it.

It will take a couple of minutes the first time but the second time it will be much quicker.

To do a test, select the protection group snapshot you want to recover. You can select any snapshot at any point in time. It defaults to the latest snapshot.

117

You can type TEST PLAN in all caps and click Run Test, as shown in Figure 2-78.

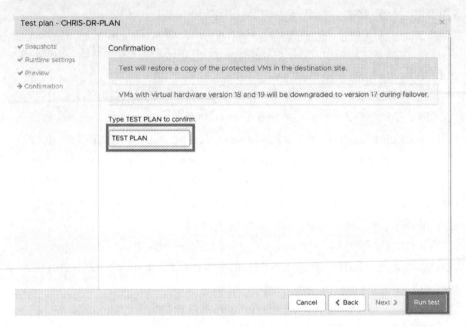

Figure 2-78. *Executing a failover test*

Once the test is over, you have to clean up the test by undoing the tasks, unregistering the VMs, and reverting back to initial state. See Figure 2-79.

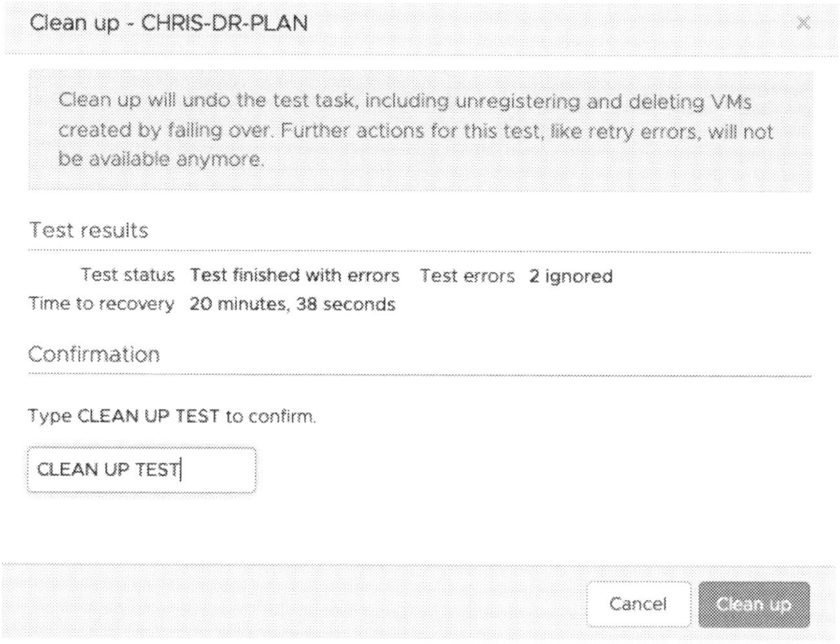

Clean up - CHRIS-DR-PLAN   ✕

Clean up will undo the test task, including unregistering and deleting VMs
created by failing over. Further actions for this test, like retry errors, will not
be available anymore.

Test results

        Test status **Test finished with errors**   Test errors **2 ignored**
Time to recovery 20 minutes, 38 seconds

Confirmation

Type CLEAN UP TEST to confirm.

CLEAN UP TEST

                                                           Cancel   Clean up

Figure 2-79. *Cleaning up a failover test*

The clean-up process will delete all the VMs from the SCFS.

Failback with DR Plans

After a failover, VMware Live Cyber Recovery does support failback
replication and migration. In fact, if your primary datacenter storage hasn't
been destroyed in the disaster, the solution brings back only changed data
from the cloud, which is a key value proposition (it greatly reduces the
time to recover and the egress costs).

If the original protected site datastore has gone, then VMWare Live
Cyber Recovery will do a full failback (and egress) of the VMs that were
originally failed over to the SDDC in VMC.

Post disaster, after the disaster has been resolved, returning to normal
operations is just as easy as falling over in the event of a disaster.

What you do is pick the plan you used to fail over to the cloud.

From the Orchestrator UI, under the DR plans view, simply select the desired plan, duplicate it, and reverse the direction. Once the new plan is created, run through the health checks to make sure that everything is ready to fail back.

You might have to make some changes to the plan or the environments depending on what happened while operating in the cloud or resolving the on-premises data center.

The health check process will give you guidance on what needs to be addressed. Then you can execute that fallback plan.

The failback process leverages change block tracking of the workloads running in the cloud to minimize the amount of data that needs to replicate back to the on-premises site through the SCFS back to the DRaaS connector.

At the end of the failback, those virtual machines are restored to the same point in time that the cloud instance was last running.

At this point, the related cloud compute resources are no longer needed, and you could choose to take advantage of cloud compute economics and reduce the cluster size in the cloud, or even eliminate this point.

It is important to note here that a failback operation is a planned activity and there will be some downtime of the applications. This will occur during the snapshot and replication stages of this process and this will depend on how much has changed during the DR operation period as well as on network bandwidth. If the datastore doesn't exist anymore, you can pick a different one.

When you commit to production to the cloud, you create a failback plan, which reverses everything in the failover plan.

When you recover to the cloud, the very first thing you do before you power the VM on into the cloud is **to take a snapshot**. Save that snapshot and utilize it as a *baseline* for recovery.

When you are ready to come back from the cloud to on-premises, you initiate that failback plan. You take that baseline you created, you power down the initial VM on the initial site, and you sync those VMs with the baseline snapshot. Once the baseline is in sync, you shut down the VM in the cloud and take another snapshot. This next snapshot is going to be a delta between the initial baseline snapshot and when you just powered it off.

You then take that snapshot and send the delta across; when it's in sync, you power on the VM on the original source site and remove the VM from the cloud.

You must configure the default datastore for recovery VM. This is useful when you choose to restore VMs back to a different location than the earlier VM. This location can be a datastore in an existing protected site or a new datastore in a new protected site. See Figure 2-80.

Commit - Pilot-recovery   ×

Commit will finish the failover task. Further actions for this task, like rollback
or retry, will not be available anymore.

Failover results

Failover status   **Failed over with no**   Errors   **None**
                  errors

         Time to   **2 minutes, 33 seconds**
        recovery

Failover notes

Failback plan

☑ **Create a failback plan**
The failback plan reverses source and destination, and the corresponding mappings.

Failback plan name

[failback] Pilot-recovery

VMware Cloud DR will attempt to fail back VMs to their original datacenter and
datastore. If there is no datastore with the same name in the failback site, or if the VM
was created in the recovery SDDC, then it will be placed in the datastore specified
below.

Default datastore

SDDC-Datacenter/datastore/Workloa... ▾

Confirmation

Type **COMMIT FAILOVER** to confirm.

COMMIT FAILOVER

                                                        Cancel   Commit

Figure 2-80. *Creating a failback plan*

Failback from an SDDC returns only changed data. There is no rehydration, and the data remains in its native compressed and deduplicated form. You must activate the plan that is created to run the failback. Once the plan is activated, you get an option to failover from the VMware Cloud on AWS SDDC. See Figure 2-81.

Figure 2-81. *Failback to a RP*

2.3.2 Alerting and Checking Compliance

Configuring alerts and compliance checks are two important setups before and during the execution of DR Plans.

Alerting

When you create a DR Plan, you can specifically set up alerting. You can define who gets the alerts, as shown in Figure 2-82.

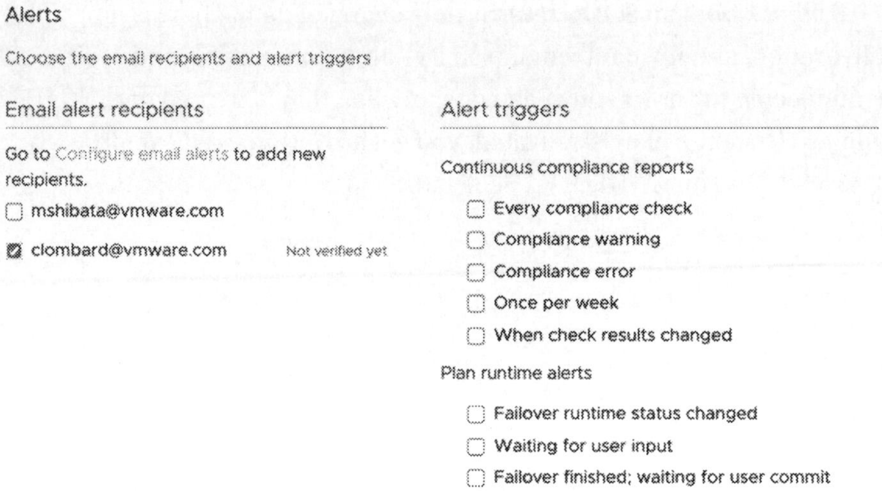

Alerts

Choose the email recipients and alert triggers

Email alert recipients

Go to Configure email alerts to add new recipients.

☐ mshibata@vmware.com

☑ clombard@vmware.com   Not verified yet

Alert triggers

Continuous compliance reports

☐ Every compliance check
☐ Compliance warning
☐ Compliance error
☐ Once per week
☐ When check results changed

Plan runtime alerts

☐ Failover runtime status changed
☐ Waiting for user input
☐ Failover finished; waiting for user commit

Figure 2-82.   Configuring alerting in a DR Plan in VLCR

- If you want to add an additional email address, click the Configure email alerts button.

- When you enter an email address, you are able to send anything right away.

Please note that VLCR uses the AWS mail service to send alerts. Recipients must respond to an email address verification request before getting email from VLCR.

You will receive a verification email (it's an AWS-branded email). You are leveraging AWS simple email service. You will receive this kind of email prior to adding your email address. See Figure 2-83.

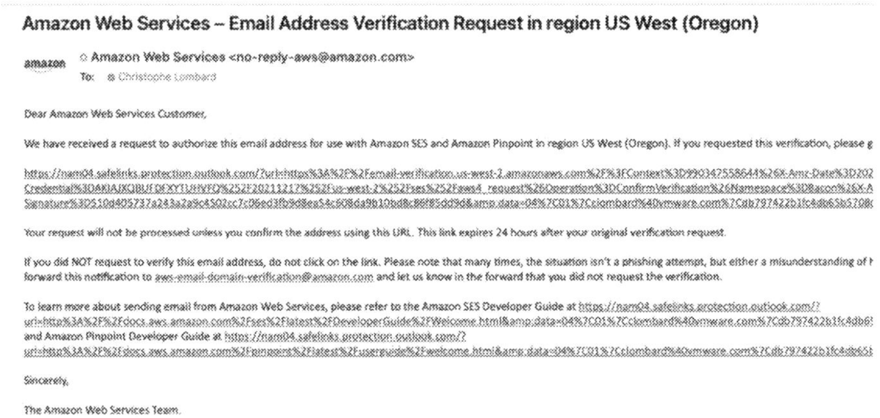

Amazon Web Services – Email Address Verification Request in region US West (Oregon)

amazon   ◇ Amazon Web Services <no-reply-aws@amazon.com>
          To: ⊗ Christophe Lombard

Dear Amazon Web Services Customer,

We have received a request to authorize this email address for use with Amazon SES and Amazon Pinpoint in region US West (Oregon). If you requested this verification, please g

https://nam04.safelinks.protection.outlook.com/?url=https%3A%2F%2Femail-verification.us-west-2.amazonaws.com%2F%3FContext%3D99034755864%26X-Amz-Date%3D202
Credential%3DAKIAJXQBUFDFXYTUHVFQ%252F20211217%252Fus-west-2%252Fses%252Faws4_request%26Operation%3DConfirmVerification%26Namespace%3D0&ason%26X-A
Signature%3DS10d405737a243a2a9c4S02cc7c06ed3fb9d8ea54c608da9b10bd8c86f85dd9d&amp.data=04%7C01%7Cclombard%40vmware.com%7Cdb797422b1fc4db65b5708(

Your request will not be processed unless you confirm the address using this URL. This link expires 24 hours after your original verification request.

If you did NOT request to verify this email address, do not click on the link. Please note that many times, the situation isn't a phishing attempt, but either a misunderstanding of ⊧
forward this notification to aws-email-domain-verification@amazon.com and let us know in the forward that you did not request the verification.

To learn more about sending email from Amazon Web Services, please refer to the Amazon SES Developer Guide at https://nam04.safelinks.protection.outlook.com/?
url=http%3A%2F%2Fdocs.aws.amazon.com%2Fses%2Flatest%2FDeveloperGuide%2FWelcome.html&data=04%7C01%7Cclombard%40vmware.com%7Cdb797422b1fc4db6‼
and Amazon Pinpoint Developer Guide at https://nam04.safelinks.protection.outlook.com/?
url=http%3A%2F%2Fdocs.aws.amazon.com%2Fpinpoint%2Flatest%2Fuserguide%2Fwelcome.html&data=04%7C01%7Cclombard%40vmware.com%7Cdb797422b1fc4db65⁇

Sincerely,

The Amazon Web Services Team.

Figure 2-83. *Email for alerting*

This service has to be opt-in. The sender email address has to be one listed as registered.

You can configure VLCR to send an email when SLA statuses change and when a recovery plan finishes running. Here are the main topics you can get alerts for:

- Continuous compliance reports (everything you configure in the plan is validated every 30 minutes)

- Plan runtime alerts

- Waiting user input is an email to let you know to acknowledge the message that the failover is finished and the program is waiting for you to commit.

Don't check "Every Compliance check" for alert triggering if it doesn't go to an automated system (it will send an email every day!). It's better to choose the "Compliance error/warning," "once per week," and "when check results changed."

Continuous Compliance Check

To make sure the failover is going to work, VLCR performs a regular compliance check. Continuous compliance checks verify the integrity of a DR Plan and ensure that any changes in the failover environment do not invalidate a DR Plan's directives when run. Compliance checks make sure that the specified Protection Groups live on the protected site and are replicating successfully to the target recovery SDDC.

Once a DR Plan is completed, the ongoing compliance checks run every half an hour. You can also execute a compliance check whenever you want by clicking the button next to Continuous compliance. See Figure 2-84.

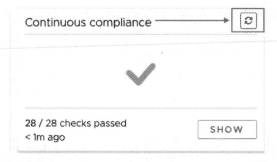

Figure 2-84. *Continuous compliance check*

The continuous compliance check is run against the DR Plan and it checks all the steps in that plan, including the mappings, including the validation of the source and the recovery environments. It does health check the source, the connector, the recovery SDDC, and it keeps track of the mappings. See Figure 2-85.

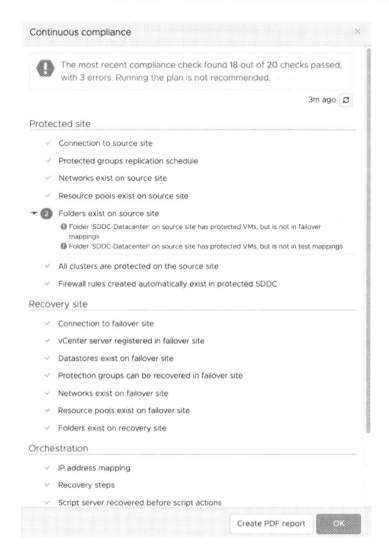

Figure 2-85. *Continuous compliance check results*

A plan can become out of compliance if any of its conditions become violated because of environmental or plan configuration changes.

It does, in a way, validate that your plan will work as designed when needed. It can also be generated as a PDF report that you can generate from the console.

2.3.3 Monitoring VMware LCR

From the UI, you can monitor all events, tasks, and alarms from all the operations going on in the system including the replication and recovery process of all your plans.

Viewing Tasks

Tasks are operations that are either running (in progress) or completed related to snapshots, SDDC creation, DR Plan execution, or system upgrades.

Tasks show the list of all running and completed tasks in the system. They are accessible from the Monitor menu on the left. See Figure 2-86.

Figure 2-86. *Monitoring – viewing tasks*

Tasks can be filtered by category (see Figure 2-87):

- Disaster recovery or ransomware operations

- **Protection**: Snapshot replication, guest file ZIP packaging for file download

- **Infrastructure**: System upgrades, cloud file system deployments

Figure 2-87. *Filtering tasks*

You can access currently running tasks from the right panel of the VMware Live Cyber Recovery UI. It also permits you to cancel some tasks and view recently completed tasks and any alarms that might be of importance.

Viewing Events

Events are an indication of an activity related to auditing, protected site operations, recovery SDDC operations, recovery of either ransomware or actual failover/test operations, or protection (snapshot operations towards the cloud filesystem). Events can inform you of a situation that requires special attention or an action to remediate an error.

The list of events shows a running list of all events from the most current to the oldest, as shown in Figure 2-88.

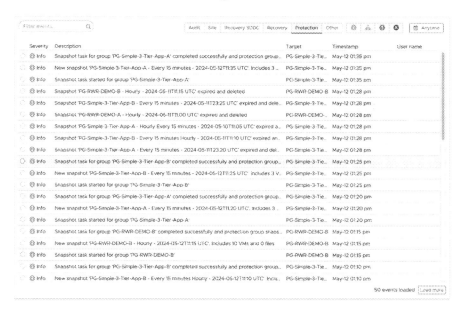

Figure 2-88. *Event list*

You can filter events if needed by

- **Category**: It can be user operations (classified as Audit), protection group and snapshot operations (Protection), protected sites (Site), recovery SDDC events, and RP failovers.

- **Severity**: It can be either Info, Warning, Error, or Emergency.

- **Specific time frame** or **event duration** like last 24 hours or last 7 days. See Figure 2-89.

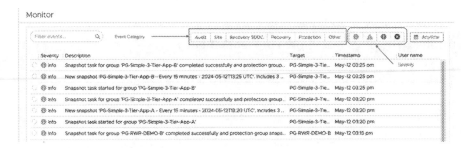

Figure 2-89. *Filtering events*

NB When you filter by event category, you cannot also filter by severity.

You can grab a specific event by clicking on it. A details panel will open and show more information about it, as shown in Figure 2-90.

Figure 2-90. *Details panel of event tasks*

A snapshot tasks type of events will generate a log when completed, which you can access by clicking the Snapshot log button in the panel below the events, as shown in Figure 2-91.

Figure 2-91. *Snapshot tasks event type*

Viewing Alarms

Alarms are notifications related to operations including all issues that require attention. Events will trigger alarms when something goes wrong and doesn't occur as planned. Alarms can only be filtered by severity, as shown in Figure 2-92.

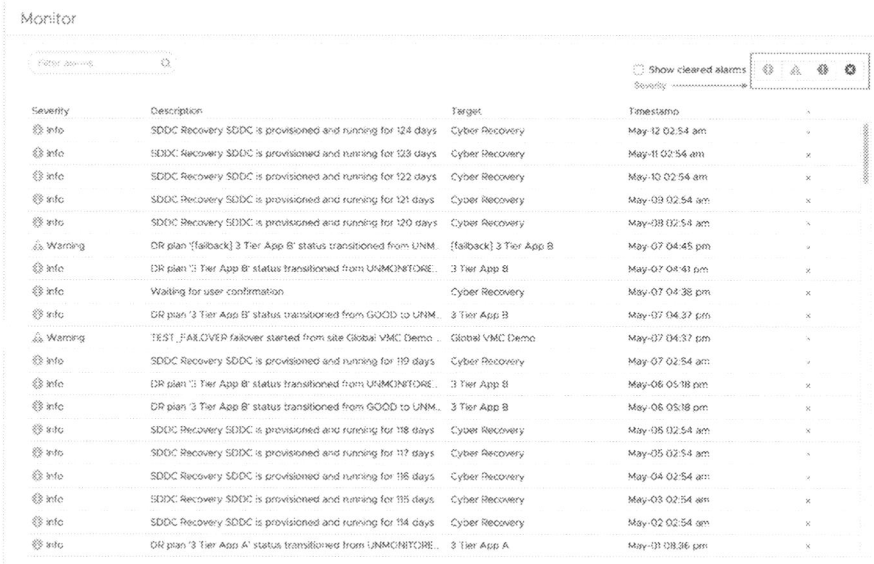

Figure 2-92. *Alarms*

Alarms can be cleared by clicking the small X on the right part of the alarm description. You revisit cleared alarms by ticking the **Show cleared alarms** box.

Checking SLA Status

The SLA status presents the administrator with visibility into the level of confidence in the DR execution by checking the status of different important bricks like protection groups, protected sites, and cloud file systems and evaluating the degree of recoverability. By default, SLA with warning or critical health will show a status banner on the dashboard. See Figure 2-93.

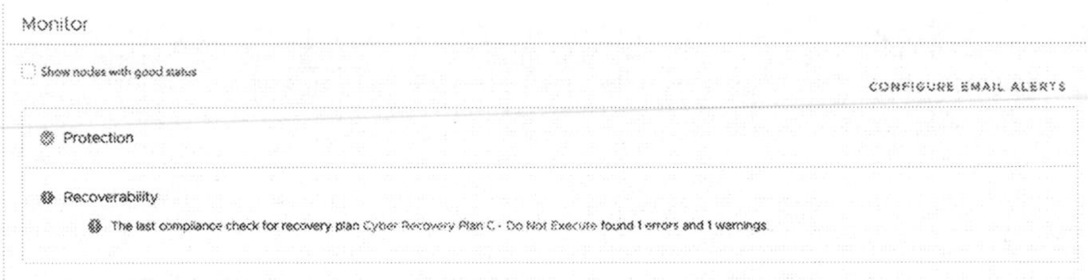

Figure 2-93. *SLA status*

You can toggle the "Show nodes with good status" button to show or hide all nodes with a good status. See Figure 2-94.

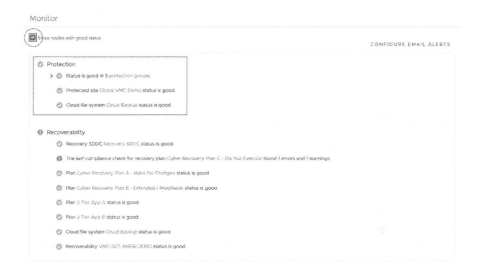

Figure 2-94. *SLA status including nodes with good status*

An SLA banner is also displayed at the top of each page. See Figure 2-95.

Figure 2-95. *SLA banner at the top of the dashboard page*

2.3.4 Reporting

VMware Cloud Disaster Recovery provides report generation in the PDF format for failover and test failover operations, plan configuration changes, and compliance checks.

Configuration Reports

The generated report contains a summary of the plan configuration, failover mapping details, and the configured failover steps. See Figure 2-96.

Protected site	Since
✓ Protection groups are healthy	Apr 25, 2024 22:01 PM UTC
✓ Folders exist on source site	Mar 26, 2024 04:09 AM UTC
✓ Connection to source site	Mar 26, 2024 04:09 AM UTC
✓ Resource pools exist on source site	Mar 26, 2024 04:09 AM UTC
✓ All clusters are protected on the source site	Mar 26, 2024 04:09 AM UTC
✓ Clusters exist in source site	Apr 9, 2024 19:30 PM UTC
✓ Firewall rules created automatically exist in protected SDDC	Apr 9, 2024 19:30 PM UTC
✓ Protected groups replication schedule	Mar 26, 2024 04:09 AM UTC
✓ Networks exist on source site	Mar 26, 2024 04:09 AM UTC

Recovery site	Since
✓ Networks exist on recovery site	Apr 18, 2024 23:31 PM UTC
✓ Resource pools exist on recovery site	Mar 26, 2024 04:09 AM UTC
✓ vCenter server registered in recovery site	Apr 9, 2024 19:30 PM UTC
✓ Connection to recovery site	Mar 26, 2024 04:09 AM UTC
✓ Clusters exist in recovery site	Apr 9, 2024 19:30 PM UTC
✓ VMs can be restored in recovery vCenter	Mar 26, 2024 04:09 AM UTC
✓ Protection groups can be recovered in recovery site	Mar 26, 2024 04:09 AM UTC
✓ Folders in protection group queries are mapped	Mar 26, 2024 04:09 AM UTC
✓ Folders exist on recovery site	Mar 26, 2024 04:09 AM UTC
✓ Datastores exist on recovery site	Mar 26, 2024 04:09 AM UTC

Orchestration	Since
✓ IP address mapping	Mar 26, 2024 04:09 AM UTC
✓ Recovery steps	Mar 26, 2024 04:09 AM UTC
✓ Script server recovered before script actions	Mar 26, 2024 04:09 AM UTC

Other	Since
✓ VMC refresh token validity	Apr 9, 2024 19:30 PM UTC
✓ VMC folder structure for file recovery is valid	Mar 26, 2024 04:09 AM UTC

Figure 2-96. *Configuration reports example*

To generate a configuration report, click the Create Report from the Continuous compliance check windows. See Figure 2-97.

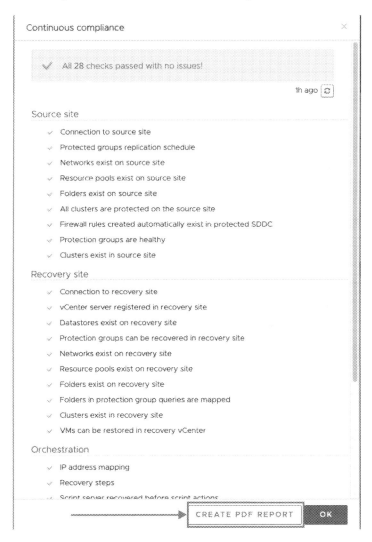

Figure 2-97. *Generating a compliance report*

Failover and Test Failover Reports

Everything that has been done during a failover or a failover test is
documented and is available through a PDF report where every step is
detailed.

You can generate a report from the DR Plan menu. Click the **Reports**
tab on a plan's details page to create the report. See Figure 2-98.

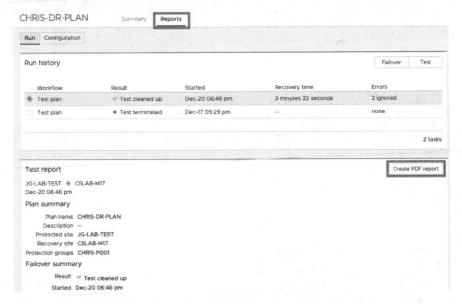

Figure 2-98. *Reports generation page*

The PDF report is autogenerated and downloaded to your local folder.
See Figure 2-99.

VMC-ORG-CSA

CHRIS-DR-PLAN

Test failover
plan runtime report

JG-LAB-TEST ➜ CSA-VCDR-SCFS

Dec 20, 2021 17:46 PM UTC

Figure 2-99.   Test failover report example

The report has multiple pages and is quite detailed as it includes the results of the tests, the plan's workflow steps, the recovery mappings, and the time that it took per VM to come up. See Figure 2-100.

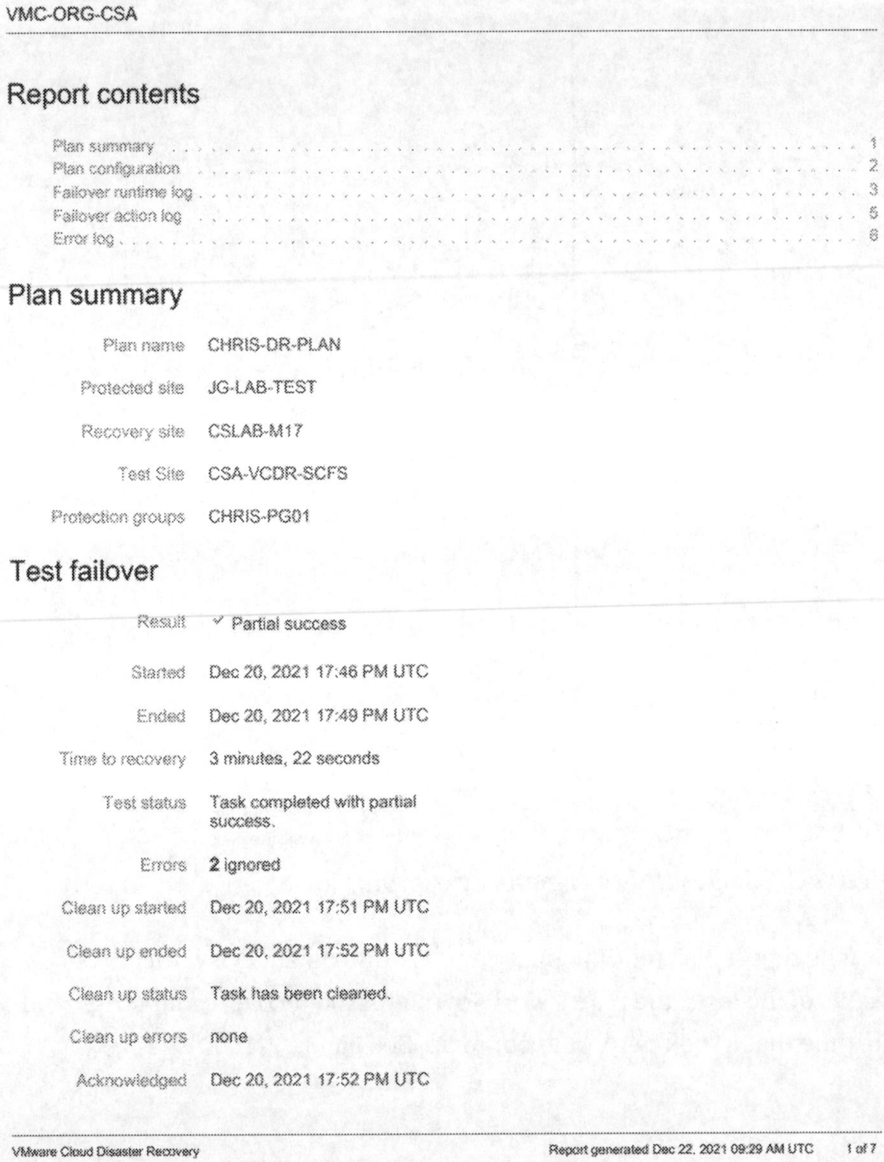

VMC-ORG-CSA

Report contents

Plan summary . . . 1
Plan configuration . . . 2
Failover runtime log . . . 3
Failover action log . . . 5
Error log . . . 6

Plan summary

Plan name	CHRIS-DR-PLAN
Protected site	JG-LAB-TEST
Recovery site	CSLAB-M17
Test Site	CSA-VCDR-SCFS
Protection groups	CHRIS-PG01

Test failover

Result	✓ Partial success
Started	Dec 20, 2021 17:46 PM UTC
Ended	Dec 20, 2021 17:49 PM UTC
Time to recovery	3 minutes, 22 seconds
Test status	Task completed with partial success.
Errors	2 ignored
Clean up started	Dec 20, 2021 17:51 PM UTC
Clean up ended	Dec 20, 2021 17:52 PM UTC
Clean up status	Task has been cleaned.
Clean up errors	none
Acknowledged	Dec 20, 2021 17:52 PM UTC

VMware Cloud Disaster Recovery   Report generated Dec 22, 2021 09:29 AM UTC   1 of 7

Figure 2-100. *Test failover report details*

The report also includes a detailed report on each action taken during the recovery operation and any errors that occurred.

Compliance Reports

You can also generate reports for the automatic compliance checks that run every 30 minutes in the system to check your DR Plans. This is a great document to share with stakeholders in charge of validation compliance inside the organization.

2.4 Summary

In this Chapter you have learnt the fundations of VMware Live Cyber Recovery, including the architecture models and the operational aspects of it. VMware Live Cyber Recovery is a SaaS-based service that leverages Cloud (VMware cloud-based managed services) as well as VMware Cloud on AWS as a recovery DR site. Deploying the solution is an easy process that will allow you to start implementing a Disaster Recovery Plan quickly and consistently with an alignement on Best practices.

To achieve your DR strategy objectives when building the VMware Live Cyber Recovery solution, you should start by deploying the main components:

- The SaaS Orchestrator
- The Scale-Out Cloud File System
- The Cyber Recovery connector

Before executing a DR Plan, you must have done the following:

- Defined a protected site where at least one connector ID deployed
- Created the protection groups with the VMs to protect and with scheduled snapshots

- Have the target recovery SDDC ready with the equivalent tags and networking configuration (prepare the segments prior to the creation of the DR plan to be able to do the network mappings)

- Documented everything that has been done during a failover or a failover test and have it available through a PDF report where every step is detailed

CHAPTER 3

Ransomware Threat and Recovery Strategies

Ransomware attacks against corporate data centers and cloud infrastructure are growing in complexity and sophistication and are challenging the readiness of data protection teams to recover from an attack. In the last year, 66% of organizations woke up to a ransomware attack. In 65% of those organizations, attackers got past the security defenses and were able to encrypt the data for ransom.

For the most part, companies have implemented a DR approach that can cover them in case of a "standard" disaster like a flood, fire, or major incident. However, the traditional approach to recover from a DR event does not work for ransomware because ransomware is a certain type of attack that requires specific features to address the complexity of recovering data in such a stressful situation. Ransomware recovery requires, for instance, more automation to guarantee the security of production workload and a shortened recovery time with limited data loss.

In this chapter, I will cover the ransomware recovery add-ons that are crucial components of the VMware Live Cyber Recovery service, and I will show how they can help enterprises address the challenge of recovering data after a ransomware.

© Christophe Lombard 2024
C. Lombard, *Mastering VMware Cloud Disaster Recovery and Ransomware Resilience,*
https://doi.org/10.1007/979-8-8688-0829-6_3

3.1 Understanding Ransomware

Once ransomware enters a system, it begins encrypting individual files or complete file systems to render them and the systems that rely on them unusable. It blocks user access until requests for payments, which are often displayed in warning messages, are fulfilled.

Unfortunately, even if the organization pays the ransom, there is no guarantee that the perpetrators will provide the cryptographic keys needed to decrypt the files.

The Cert common attack paths of a human-operated ransomware incident based on examples CERT NZ has seen are represented in Figure 3-1.

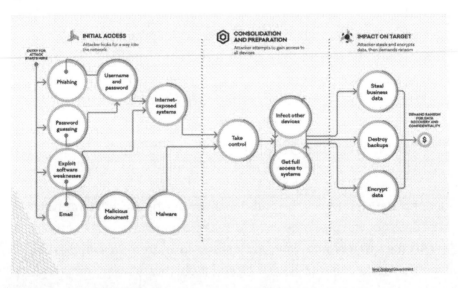

Figure 3-1. *Ransomware recovery workflow*

In the above schema, you can see that the bad actors use different techniques and tactics to get access to and infect an information system. Like any cyber-attack, a ransomware attack follows a well-established (and smart!) path with the following stages:

1. Research, identification, and selection of the target

2. **Exploitation and initial access**: It sometimes starts by a phishing attack to collect the username and password or an exploitation of software vulnerabilities. Hackers also rely more and more on advanced forms of social engineering to get access.

3. **Consolidation and preparation**: This is where the bad actor escalates its privilege and establishes remote access control to systems. It establishes its persistence.

    It can also execute actions across the network and install rootkit and malware on multiple systems.

4. **Command and control**: This is when the counter measures have failed and impact on the target starts. Ransomware encrypts a victim's files or entire system, rendering them inaccessible. Attackers then demand a ransom, usually in cryptocurrency, to provide the decryption key. The bad actor can also start destroying the backups or deactivate the DR solution. At this time, it's too late. It's done!

3.1.1 Types of Ransomware Attacks

In recent years we have witnessed an increased level of sophistication in attacks, and malicious actors have adjusted their tactics to be more destructive and impactful. Hackers have moved from a file-based approach type to attacks where traditional antivirus with a signature was usually sufficient to a "fileless" method where attacks get more invisible and require more sophisticated solutions with behavioral analysis capabilities like EDR or XDR.

Ransomware is the disaster of the decade. Ransomware attacks have evolved from scattered threats by small-time hackers into multi-stage, targeted campaigns from sophisticated criminal organizations and state-sponsored groups. Attackers today have quite a different modus operandi than they used to.

In the past, customers have addressed what I call "Ransomware 1.0" by having backups, offsite copies, immutability, air-gapping to preserve snapshot availability, and traditional file scanning to find clean restore points. These capabilities become table stakes and are not enough to address today's challenges with "Modern Ransomware," the next generation of ransomware strains. See Figure 3-2.

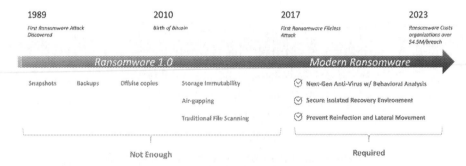

Figure 3-2. *The evolution of ransomware attacks*

These new ransomware strains live off the land, using existing tools and software that is preloaded on the operating system. We see security folks talking about "fileless attacks" where the bad actors use legitimate programs to infect the system. They're working in-memory, they're reducing or hijacking PowerShell scripts, they do not rely on files, and they leave no footprint—making it challenging to detect and remove.

These attacks are the most common forms of attacks today; 60-70% of attacks today are fileless. There are no malicious files sitting on the drive for you to scan for, so the only way you can find that is if you power up the VM in an isolate the environment so that it doesn't infect your production environment, and you leverage next-gen antivirus and behavioral analysis on that powered-on VM to look for the malicious behavior. These capabilities are now required to recover from modern ransomware.

3.1.2 The Impact of Ransomware on Organizations

Let's have a look at the challenges faced by organizations when dealing with a ransomware attack.

- The first challenge that customers may face is the limited number of snapshot history. Ransomware can dwell and continue to propagate in a customer's environment for an extended period. This makes recovering from a ransomware attack particularly challenging. Oftentimes the ransomware dwell time is longer than the snapshot history or that the backups were deleted.

- Secondly, when staging and validating recovery points, in order to prevent reinfection of the production workloads at recovery, customers need to work in a dedicated, secure, sandboxed or quarantined environment. The industry term for this is isolated recovery environment (IRE). This is the first thing that customers need to do, and customers are now building, securing, and managing their own IRE, which is a time-consuming and manual effort. Traditional backup solutions often lack an IRE, so users must build and maintain this special environment manually.

- Third, customers need to find a good snapshot candidate to start with. And if they have appropriately set up their retention schedule and have snapshots going back several months, they're potentially looking at thousands of snapshots, and finding a good place to start can be a daunting task. Oftentimes they need to rely on their security team to know which restore point to recover from, which elongates the ransomware recovery process, when every minute counts.

- Next, as mentioned, customers these days need modern security tools with next-gen AV and behavioral analysis that can analyze the behavior of running workloads, in order to pick up on next-gen ransomware strains and thereby properly validate the recovery points. Many customers still rely on traditional file scanning tools, which are ineffective at detecting these ransomware strains, and must bring in separate tools or external experts who use their own tools to validate the recovery points.

- Whenever customers only have a few options as to how to restore, such as full VM restore only, data loss becomes a real challenge.

Many customers who have been through a ransomware attack report that this was a long, painful, and complex process. A Wall Street firm said it took them 6 weeks to recover. Some customers had services that were down for 3+ months.

3.1.3 Preventing Ransomware

To limit the likelihood of being attacked by a ransomware, you need first to implement security best practices:

- Regularly update and patch software and systems.

- Implement strong access controls and regularly review permissions.

- Use encryption for sensitive data at all stages (at rest, in transit, and during processing).

- Leverage security services, such as identity and access management tools.

- Conduct regular security audits, vulnerability assessments, and penetration testing.

- Establish incident response plans and conduct regular drills.

The America's Cyber Defense Agency published the **#StopRansomware Guide**[1], which is the one-stop resource to help organizations reduce the risk of ransomware through best practices to detect, prevent, respond, and recover, including step-by-step approaches.

The recommendations align with the Cybersecurity Performance Goals (CPGs)[2] developed by CISA and the National Institute of Standards and Technology (NIST).

In a nutshell, the recommendations to limit the risks posed by ransomware and to drive a coordinated and efficient response for your organization are the following:

- Maintain offline, encrypted backups of critical data and test the availability and integrity of your backups.

- Create, maintain, and regularly exercise your Incident and Response Plan (IRP).

---

[1] www.cisa.gov/sites/default/files/2023-10/StopRansomware-Guide-508C-v3_1.pdf

[2] www.cisa.gov/cross-sector-cybersecurity-performance-goals

- Implement a zero-trust architecture.

- Do not expose services such RDP on the web.

The response checklist is quite interesting as it gives guidance on how to respond when you are a victim of ransomware and which responses to add to your IRP.

The best practices are the following:

- Identification of the systems that have been impacted

- Isolation of the systems

- Triage of impacted systems for restoration and recovery

- Log collection for evidence (this means you can't destroy the workloads that were infected)

- Reporting and notification

For VMware, a good solid recovery plan with a well-established process is the best way to recover after a disaster such as ransomware.

Here are some of the key capabilities required to implement the best ransomware recovery solution:

- Secure immutable backup copies. It's also a best practice to have the backup copies operationally air-gapped and immutable to prevent modification.

- **Deep history of backup copies**: Keeping at least three months of data is a best practice when recovering from ransomware as the dwell time can be very long.

- Have a dedicated workflow with guided restore point selection to facilitate the selection of the right point in time copy.

- Have a rapid iteration of the snapshots to quickly iterate and find the right candidates for restoration.

- Behavioral analysis of the workloads to remove malware during the recovery iteration

- IRE and isolation of the VM during the recovery process to prevent malware lateral movement in the IRE. It's crucial to not reinfect clean systems during recovery.

3.2 VMware Cyber Recovery Ransomware approach

3.2.1 Ransomware Recovery vs. Disaster Recovery

When you are hit by ransomware, the situation is very different from a traditional DR event. The reason why is because in this case your production environment is still alive, but a subset of the data is encrypted and inaccessible. The goal is to get them back in operations.

Relying on the DR workflow won't be efficient enough as it will bring all the virtual machines from the same point in time. Ransomware has a dwell time; it takes a while in your environment and spreads out, establishing command and control while cataloging vulnerabilities. Recovering multiple workloads from the same point-in-time is not helpful. Some machines may have been infected some weeks ago, some may have been infected days ago. Some of them were never infected prior to being encrypted. So, machines that are still clean can be reinfected.

During a ransomware attack, you cannot manage it the same way. It requires a specific workflow to tackle the challenge of ransomware recovery. First of all, you need a process for finding and validating the best recovery points through an iterative workflow. Secondly, you need to be able to perform rapid recovery tasks in a controlled environment to minimize the overall recovery time and the risk of reinfection. It may be necessary to iterate across many snapshots in the protection schedules to find the best candidate VM(s) to proceed with. This iterative workflow should offer partial recovery of subsets of protected VM. This can be facilitated by using a simple interface to help you find the best point in time to restart each virtual machine based on some criteria.

During the ransomware recovery process, your objective is to recover compromised workloads and minimize the loss of data while providing data integrity and security assurance.

The ransomware recovery process can be accomplished only if some preparation has been done to make sure everything is ready to run as needed. For instance, an appropriate retention period must be chosen for the specific case of ransomware. A longer snapshot retention time should be selected to address the potential dwell time (duration between the infection and when the ransomware did activate). The protection group where you place your workloads should reflect the appropriate schedule and retention time. VMware recommends at least three months for the retention when dealing with a ransomware recovery.

To avoid reinfecting the production environment and to keep track of the infected workload for forensic analysis, it is preferable to be able to recover the production VMs to a different environment on a separate network. These production VMs could be failed back to the production environment once it has been cleaned up.

3.2.2 Overview of VMware Cyber Recovery Ransomware Add-On

In the following chapter you have also learned how VLCR can address Ransomware Threats through a well established workflow. VMware Live Cyber Recovery leverages core capabilities and features to provide the ideal last line of defense to recover from ransomware with a set of tools and environment. Let's have a look at them:

- **True air-gapped, immutable recovery point file system**: No access points, no NFS mount, no FS to browse. Data goes into the native application and is stored in immutable format because there is never an overwrite. In addition, it uses a log structured file system that is totally air-gapped. No one can browse and no one can delete the data.

- **Instant power-on**: No other cloud backup vendor can do this: any backup, at any point in time, can be turned on instantly without any data rehydration and zero copy. Any snapshots can be turned on and registered in the recovery SDDC running in the cloud in a matter of seconds. This gives a great capability to iterate. There is automation to power off; bring up and try the next one.

- **Deep snapshot history**: With VMware Cloud Disaster Recovery, it is possible to keep a wide variety and retention of recovery points to draw from. It offers a deep snapshot history from hours, days, even up to months, and you can recover all of these snapshots without any RTO penalty. This is clearly important when you want to make sure you can recover your data before the bad code lands on your system. See Figure 3-3.

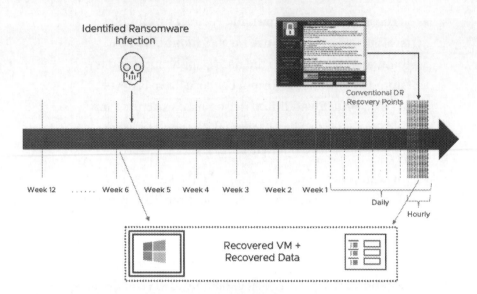

Figure 3-3. *Ransomware recovery of data process*

This is critical if simply rolling back in time to a
recent clean recovery point is not possible. It is
possible to bring more recent, still accessible VM
instances into inventory, set them aside, and then
copy their data into a clean VM recovery instance
from an earlier point in time, potentially even before
any attack was present.

- **A dedicated IRE**: VMWare Cloud on AWS SDDC as the
  core recovery site is an ideal solution to recover from
  ransomware and it can be deployed just in time with
  a minimal size and can take advantage of the cloud
  scalability. NSX Advanced Firewall is also included in
  the service, and it is fully automated. It offers features
  needed for basic network management like compute
  gateway, distributed firewalls, and security features to

protect the workloads running inside the IRE. Every machine gets started in a totally isolated mode where it can't talk to anything and it can't be accessed.

- **Next-generation antivirus for workload analysis**: Another service available with the service is Carbon Black Cloud Endpoint and Workload Protection. This provides an advanced security solution to control the level of security in the workloads that need to be recovered and remove the latest modern threats in the running workloads. The behavioral analysis embedded in the solution helps detect more sophisticated attacks. This is a true differentiator to detect and remediate the ransomware malware type of attacks.

We will look more closely at how the features and capabilities of VLCR get implemented later in this book.

3.2.3 How VLCR Addresses Ransomware Threats

In the previous sections, you saw that VMware Live Cyber Recovery provides a set of capabilities that are dedicated to addressing the ransomware recovery case. Now let see the ransomware recovery workflow and tasks you need to follow to address the challenge of recovering your data.

Ransomware Recovery Process and Steps

One of the first customer challenges in ransomware recovery is **identifying the right recovery point** candidates. This can be a daunting task as there are going to be a lot of snapshots to look at. And it's very difficult to know when your system was infected or encrypted.

The next step after deciding which restore point to pick is **validating the restore point**. How do you know if this restore point is good? Maybe it's not encrypted, but how do you know if the bad actor is still there? Maybe it's not encrypted but what if the bad actors are still on the machine or if you stood up a restore point that still has the malicious code?

In addition, to avoid reinfection, VMs need to be evaluated in an **isolated environment**, which can be complex to set up and maintain.

To address those key challenges of the ransomware recovery, VLCR has very powerful capabilities that are truly different from any other vendors.

VMware Live Cyber Recovery offers a well-defined workflow that will guide you during the process. To address the process of recovering from a ransomware with VLCR, you must follow these steps:

1. Prepare for the ransomware recovery.

2. Run a Recovery Plan that has been enabled for ransomware recovery.

3. Start validating the VMs from snapshots in the isolated environment

4. Iterate the security analysis and remediation.

5. Stage the validated VMs.

6. Recover VMs to the protected site.

7. End the recovery process.

Enabling Ransomware Recovery

The ransomware recovery service has to be enabled from the Recovery Plan. The first thing you need to enable is the integrated analysis in your Recovery Plan. See Figure 3-4.

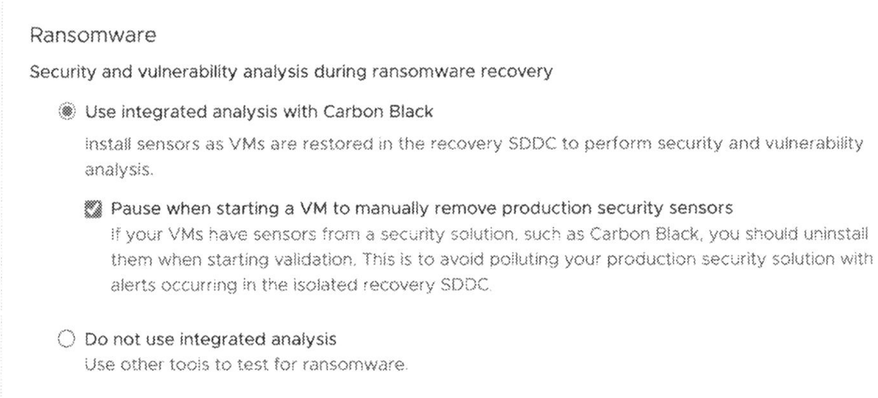

Ransomware

Security and vulnerability analysis during ransomware recovery

○ Use integrated analysis with Carbon Black

Install sensors as VMs are restored in the recovery SDDC to perform security and vulnerability analysis.

☑ Pause when starting a VM to manually remove production security sensors

If your VMs have sensors from a security solution, such as Carbon Black, you should uninstall them when starting validation. This is to avoid polluting your production security solution with alerts occurring in the isolated recovery SDDC.

○ Do not use integrated analysis

Use other tools to test for ransomware.

Figure 3-4. *Ransomware recovery service activation*

You can select the country in which you would like data analysis to take place when you enable integrated security and vulnerability analysis. Moreover, VMware Live Cyber Recovery installs a Carbon Black Cloud Workload VM on the recovery SDDC when you enable integrated security and vulnerability analysis. This VM controls communication between Carbon Black Cloud servers and VMware Live Cyber Recovery.

VMware Live Cyber Recovery leverages NSX Advanced Firewall to enforce advanced network isolation levels inside the recovery SDDC. You may allow VMware Live Cyber Recovery to automatically activate the feature only during ransomware recovery or testing.

The procedure to enable the service is as follows:

- From the left navigation, select **Settings.**

- Under Integration, click **Ransomware Recovery Services.** See Figure 3-5.

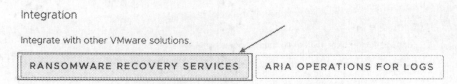

Integration

Integrate with other VMware solutions.

| RANSOMWARE RECOVERY SERVICES | ARIA OPERATIONS FOR LOGS |

Figure 3-5. *Ransomware recovery service activation*

- Click the Activate Integrated Analysis button.

- Select the country and confirm each of the items and click **Activate.**

- You can now activate NSX Advanced FW by clicking **Allow Activation of Advanced FW.**

- Confirm and acknowledge the statements and click **Activate.** See Figure 3-6.

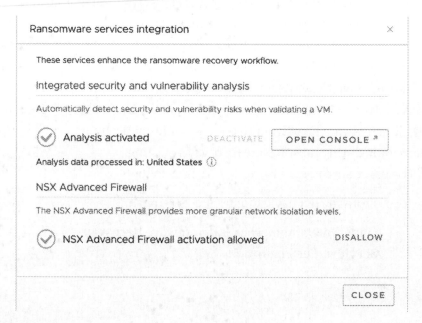

Figure 3-6. *Ransomware service activation*

A Dedicated Ransomware Recovery Workflow

When you are experiencing ransomware and going into the process of recovering from it, above all, there is a task which can be very time consuming, which is the creation of a workflow or a runbook when you realize that you have been attacked.

VMware Live Cyber Recovery offers you the ability to be guided through the recovery process by providing a **dedicated workflow**. This is an important feature from a time-saving perspective especially during that stressful time.

This workflow provides the ability to run a specific dedicated Recovery Plan for ransomware recovery that includes multiple tasks. When executing these tasks, the VMs move through three stages: **In validation**, **Staged**, and **Recovered**. At the beginning of the process, each VM starts in the "in backup" stage. See Figure 3-7.

Figure 3-7. *Ransomware recovery summary*

During the first step, you move the VM snapshots from the "**in backup**" stage to the "**in validation**" stage. It means that you start them into the recovery SDDC environment to validate them. It's recommend to have a few hosts in the VMware cloud on AWS as a pilot light environment to facilitate the iterations. VMs are started from a NFS datastore that is automatically presented through a live mount feature to the recovery SDDC.

At this stage, you have the choice to select individual VMs or a set of VMs in the inventory and process them through the guided workflow.

The criteria to select VMs are based on VM name, group membership, and the current guided recovery workflow state. You can search for VMs from the VM list. As you can see in Figure 3-8, you can select all VMs in the "in backup" state.

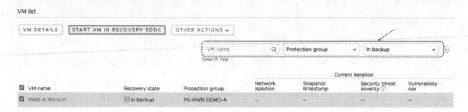

Figure 3-8. *Selecting VMs in bulk for ransomware recovery*

NB   Bulk operations are limited to 50 VMs per selection, per action.

When you start a VM in validation, it is considered an iteration. You can iterate VMs in validation as many times as you want by selecting different snapshots.

When you have finished selecting the right VMs, select the option **Validate in Recovery SDDC**. See Figure 3-9.

Figure 3-9. *Moving to the "in validation" step*

To select the right snapshot, you will be presented with the snapshot timeline to analyze snapshot change rate and entropy rate to validate your choice. You will be able to try different snapshots for VMs before you grab the one with the highest probability to be encrypted, which is the one that has the least amount of entropy and a higher rate of compression. See Figure 3-10.

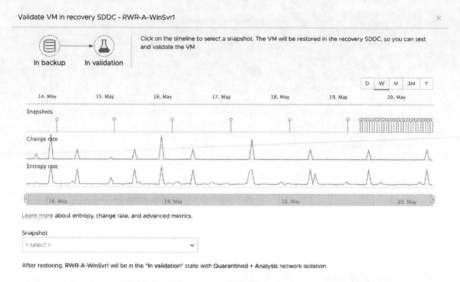

Figure 3-10. *Snapshot timeline*

Just after clicking the Validation button, VMware Live Recovery will use the **live mount** feature to instantly power on the selected VM snapshots in a quarantine state (snapshots will be isolated from each other). Live mount means the ability for hosts in VMware Cloud on AWS to boot VMs directly from snapshots stored securely in the SCFS, which is backed by cloud native storage.

After, if you opt-in for the integrated security scanning, it will automatically install a security sensor (Carbon Black agent) on Windows VMs (manually on Linux VMs) and immediately begin performing a behavior analysis on the running machines as well as a malware and vulnerability scan. Behavioral analysis should run for a longer period of time. It will continue running for a recommended minimum of 8 hours. This will help prevent recovering infected virtual machines back to production. See Figure 3-11.

Figure 3-11. *Security and vulnerability scanning*

During that stage, you will be able to monitor the security events and alerts generated by the scan, change the isolation level, restore files from other snapshots, and review the snapshot timeline to analyze the **change rate** and **entropy level** (see below for the explanation). This will help you decide if the snapshot can be approved for production or not. See Figure 3-12.

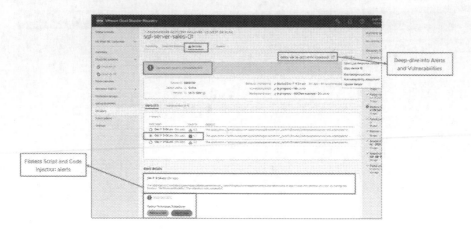

Figure 3-12. *Vulnerability alerts from scanning*

If you think that the snapshot still presents a risk of hosting malicious code or that there is encrypted content, you can badge the snapshot to quickly identify the infected snapshots. See Figure 3-13.

Figure 3-13. *Badging a snapshot*

It is possible to assign a predefined badge to any recovery point under consideration. Snapshot badges are user-applied attributes and they can be assigned a predefined value from the list shown in Figure 3-14 and below:

◉	❓	Not badged	No information on the status of this snapshot
○	✅	Verified	This snapshot is safe
○	⚠️	Warning	There are concerns about this snapshot
○	❗	Compromised	Malware detected
○	❌	Encrypted	Data encrypted

Figure 3-14. *Snapshots badges*

- **Not badged**: No information on the security status

- **Verified**: It means snapshot is considered safe.

- **Warning**: Some of the data of the snapshot might be compromised.

- **Compromised**: The snapshot has some vulnerabilities and malware infection.

- **Encrypted**: Data in the snapshot has been encrypted.

At that stage you can consider the snapshot as compromised and restart a validation process again from a different snapshot.

If you decide the VM snapshot is not compromised, you can move it to the **staged** stage. The system will then power off the validated VM and take a snapshot of it to prepare it for recovery to the protected site. For Windows VM, the security sensor will be automatically removed. For Linux VM, you will have to uninstall it prior to the staging phase.

Guest File Restore

VMware Live Cyber Recovery offers that capability to recover certain files with a guest file restore utility. This permits adding more recent data from an alternate recovery point into an older recovery point that has been selected as clean.

The utility itself offers to view VM file content of a specific recovery point in time and extra specific files or directories from those snapshots into a local location. The extracted files are presented as a ZIP archive that can be downloaded, unpacked, and merged into a working recovery copy of a VM. See Figure 3-15.

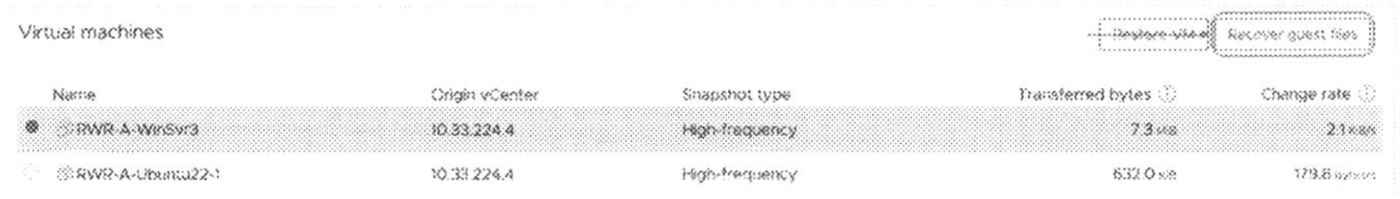

Figure 3-15. *Guest file restore option*

After the guest files have been updated, it's a good practice to relaunch a security scanning to make sure the VM is clean before you recover it back to production.

You can send a link to the guest file to other users from **Monitor** > **Tasks**. See Figure 3-16.

Figure 3-16. *Guest file restore from the Tasks menu*

NB   If you are limiting access to the VLCR UI, only the IP addresses that are listed under the access list can download the guest files for recovery.

You can recover guest files from three different locations:

- The virtual machine list

- A snapshot inside a protection group

- The **Other** menu during the ransomware recovery process when VMs are in the validation state

The procedure to restore files from a VM is as follow:

- From the left navigation, select **Virtual Machines.**

- Grab the VM you want to recover files from and click **Recover Guest files.** See Figure 3-17.

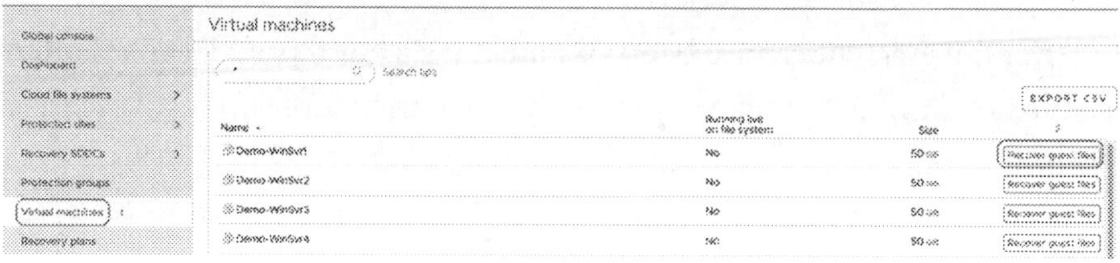

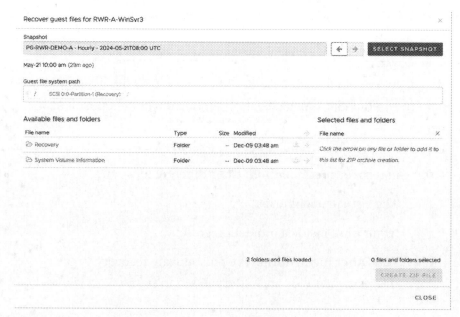

Figure 3-17. *Restoring a guest file from the VM list*

If you are using a protection group to select the VM, select the PG and then the snapshot before selecting the VM.

From the **Select snapshot dialog**, select the snapshot you want to use, as shown in Figure 3-18.

Figure 3-18. *Selecting a snapshot for guest file restore*

The virtual disks analysis starts, as shown in Figure 3-19.

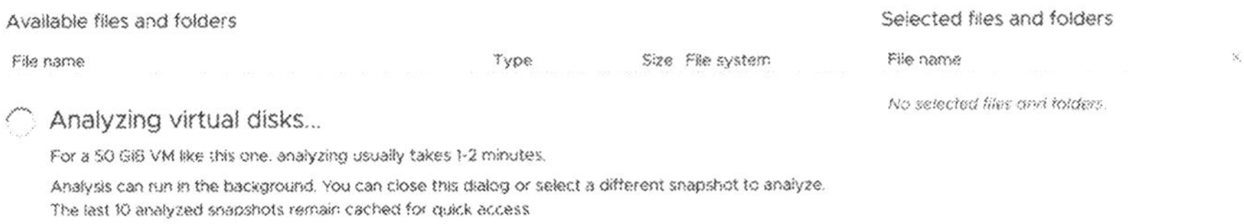

Available files and folders

File name   Type   Size File system

◯ Analyzing virtual disks...

For a 50 GiB VM like this one, analyzing usually takes 1-2 minutes.

Analysis can run in the background. You can close this dialog or select a different snapshot to analyze.
The last 10 analyzed snapshots remain cached for quick access.

Selected files and folders

File name   ×

No selected files and folders

Figure 3-19. *Disk analysis for guest files restore*

After a couple of minutes, the partition with directories is displayed, as shown in Figure 3-20.

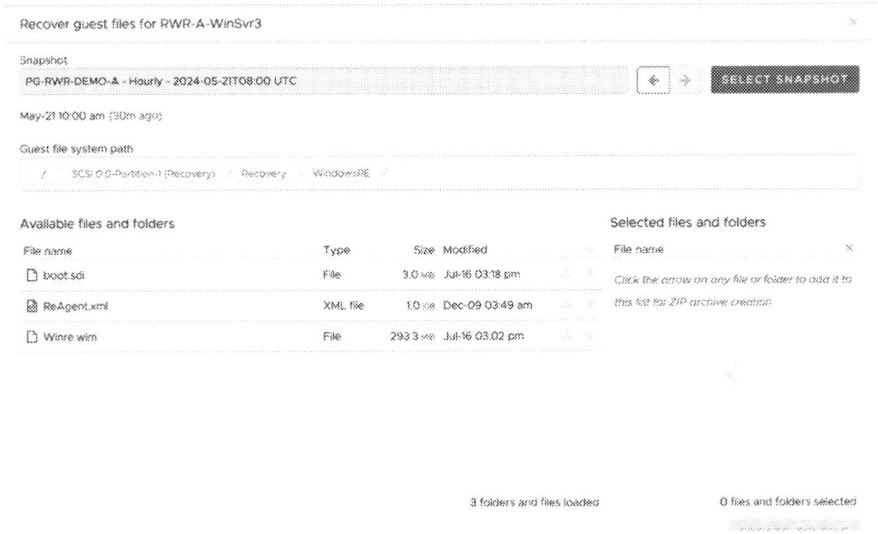

Recover guest files for RWR-A-WinSvr3   ×

Snapshot

PG-RWR-DEMO-A - Hourly - 2024-05-21T08:00 UTC   ←   →   SELECT SNAPSHOT

May-21 10:00 am (30m ago)

Guest file system path

/ SCSI 0:0-Partition-1 (Recovery) / Recovery / WindowsPE /

Available files and folders

File name   Type   Size Modified   Selected files and folders

📄 boot.sdi   File   3.0 kB Jul-16 03:18 pm   File name   ×

📄 ReAgent.xml   XML file   1.0 kB Dec-09 03:49 am   Click the arrow on any file or folder to add it to
                                                                           this list for ZIP archive creation.
📄 Winre.wim   File   293.3 kB Jul-16 03:02 pm

                                               3 folders and files loaded   0 files and folders selected

Figure 3-20. *VM disk partition for guest file recovery*

Once the VM has loaded, select the file(s) you want and click the arrow on the left to download a ZIP package with the files. See Figure 3-21.

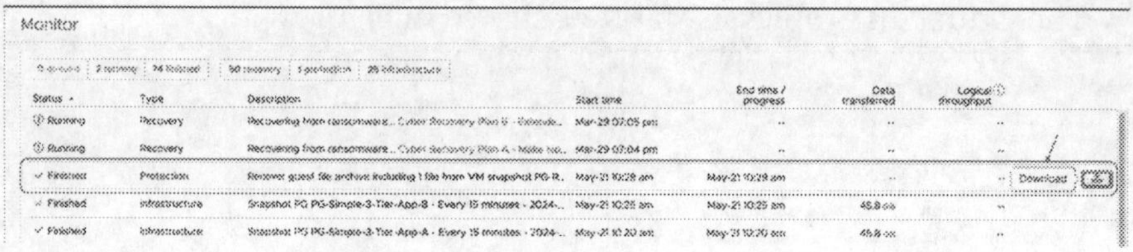

Figure 3-21. *Downloading a guest file*

After the ZIP file downloads, click Close. Your user must have file-level permissions to unzip the package.

Guided Restore Point Selection

VMware Live Cyber Recovery offers a dedicated interface that is able to show you, through a graphical view of your VM, when is the most likely and best point in time to restart each virtual machine based on specific metrics like compressibility and change rate that can be combined with data you have from your IDS or forensics that have been done.

This means whenever you have that sea of snapshots to select from where to begin, VMware Live Cyber Recovery offers you guidance on which snapshots potentially are encrypted, so that you don't lose time selecting those that are encrypted or compromised.

This is on the snapshot timeline that appears when you first start VMs **in validation** stage and select from the **Timeline** tab and when you try a different snapshot during the validation process. See Figure 3-22.

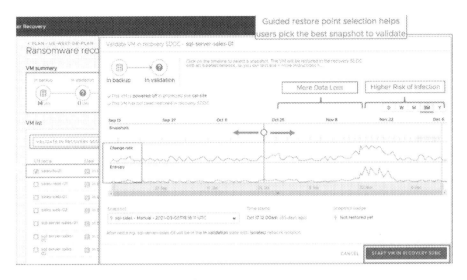

Figure 3-22. *Snapshot timeline*

Let's say there has been an encryption through malware. The guided workflow will help you pull the VMs into a guided restore point selection where you will be able to check two different metrics: change rate and entropy level.

Change rate is the number of bytes changed that you divide by the time difference between the current snapshot and the previous snapshot.

The entropy level is a metric measuring the level of consistency between files in the disks. This is based on the calculation of the entropy rate, which corresponds to the following formula: 1/compression ratio. The entropy rate is a number between 0 and 1, and the closer it is to 1, the higher the likelihood the snapshot has been encrypted. Sudden jumps in entropy level are a clear indication of a possible encryption.

Both metrics are calculated and displayed in the Timeline tab when you select a VM for testing. See Figure 3-23.

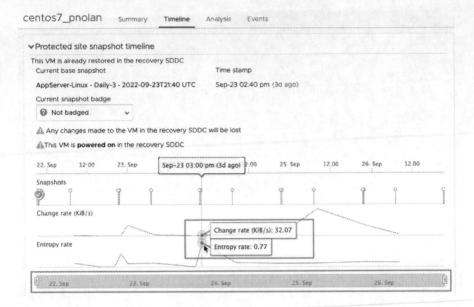

Figure 3-23. *Change rate and entropy level in the timeline*

When VMware Live Cyber Recovery detects higher change and entropy rates, it can indicate that a ransomware attack encrypting the data is ongoing or has happened. It is then recommended to pick the snapshot before the onset of malware activity as it may contain unencrypted data.

Once you have decided on the version of the snapshot you want to start, within 30 seconds the machine will power up in the recovery SDDC without access to the external world.

Isolated Environment and Network Isolation

Another important differentiator is that you can provision an on-demand IRE (a quarantined or sandboxed environment) on VMware Cloud on AWS for testing and validating the recovery points.

VMware Cloud on AWS SDDC works very well as an isolated environment, and it offers a great on-demand option to help save money. You have the choice to consume it on-demand or as a Pilot Light to have two nodes minimum waiting for the DR event to happen. The Pilot Light option is a better option when you are looking for the lowest RTO.

With VMware Cloud on AWS is a "safe" place to spin up VMs to prevent your production environment from seeing reinfection; it's a true sandbox environment.

Having this dedicated, secure environment for validation and testing is critical for preventing reinfection of the production workloads, and you can bring this up on-demand, as a fully VMware-managed environment.

Additionally, you have push-button VM network isolation levels that allow you to easily assign network isolation policies to VMs to prevent lateral movement of the malware within the IRE. This is possible using NSX Advanced Firewall within VMware Cloud on AWS SDDC. You get a push button method with seven preconfigured isolation levels to take all the work out of the administrator from totally quarantine to totally open. See Figure 3-24.

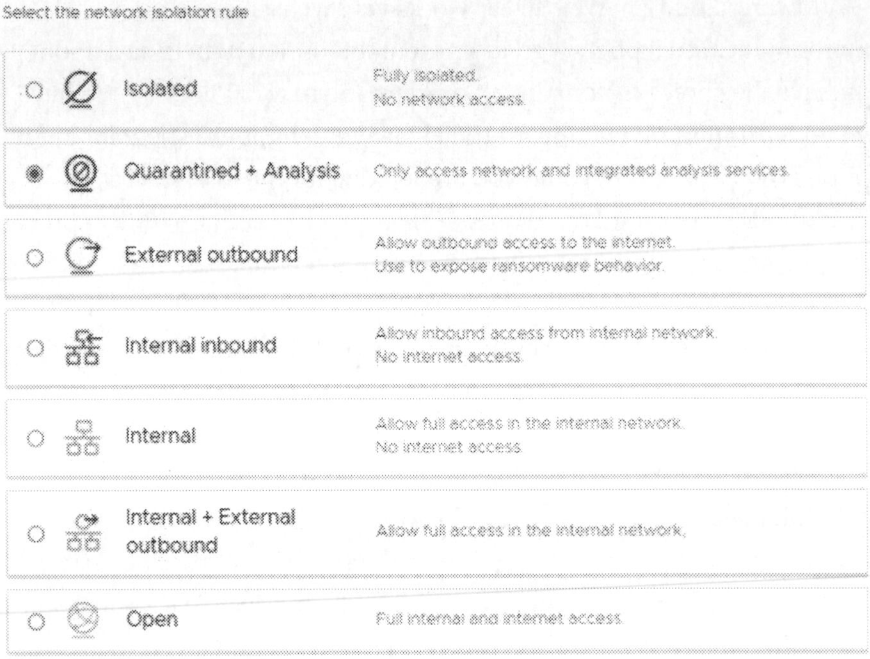

Select the network isolation rule

○	⦰	Isolated	Fully isolated. No network access.
●	◎	Quarantined + Analysis	Only access network and integrated analysis services.
○	↻	External outbound	Allow outbound access to the internet. Use to expose ransomware behavior.
○	品	Internal inbound	Allow inbound access from internal network. No internet access.
○	品	Internal	Allow full access in the internal network. No internet access.
○	品	Internal + External outbound	Allow full access in the internal network.
○	⊘	Open	Full internal and internet access.

Figure 3-24. *Network isolation levels*

Please note that when a VM is initially brought into the IRE, it always start in isolation mode (Quarantine + Analysis) which means the VM can only connect over the internet to the NGAV Tools (integrated security and vulnerability servers on Carbon Black Cloud) and to basic network services like DNS and NTP. All other north/south or east/west network traffic is limited through NSX Firewall rules.

Changing the isolation is always possible by changing the network isolation rule through a push-button selection option.

Behavior Analysis and Remediation

Modern malware isn't just files on servers that you can scan. It requires a next-generation antivirus that does behavioral analysis, not just file-level inspection. Inspection of powered-on workloads in isolation with embedded Next-Gen AV (NGAV) and behavior analysis helps detect abnormal activities like changes to executables or Zero Day viruses.

This is another great differentiator. Look at competitive offerings and see how scanning of snapshots is realized. Hackers know exactly how scanning for a file signature can be easily avoided. They do avoid it. Whenever bad guys go after systems they use fileless method: they work in memory and they elevate their privileges.

In order to know if a virtual machine is exhibiting a bad behavior, during the boot process, when you start a VM in ransomware recovery on the recovery SDDC, a next-generation antivirus (Carbon Black) uses ML/AI scans for known vulnerabilities and for malware signatures. In addition, a deep behavior analysis of all running software and processes on the VM guest OS begins, looking for suspicious behavior.

When you run a ransomware recovery plan, the Carbon Black sensor is automatically installed on Windows VMs if the Recovery Plan is enabled for integrated security and vulnerability analysis and if VMware Tools version 11.2 or later is installed on the VM. See Figure 3-25.

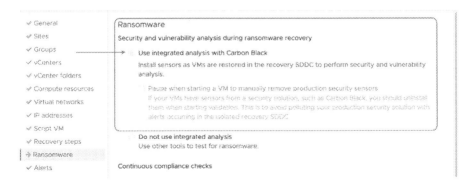

Figure 3-25. *Integrated analysis selection in DR Plan*

For Linux VMs, the Carbon Black launcher is not included into the VMware Tools so it must be installed manually.

You can inspect OS and application vulnerabilities from the integrated analysis.

The **Vulnerability** tab shows a list of all found vulnerabilities with their CVE number and a link to the vulnerability article in the National Institute of Standards and Technology (NIST) database. See Figure 3-26.

Figure 3-26. *Vulnerabilities results from analysis*

Once the vulnerability scanning completes, you can remediate them by patching the VM directly from the IRE and executing a new scan once the remediation is completed.

The behavioral analysis is conducted in parallel, and it analyzes VMs and their guest files for abnormal behaviors like processes that make outbound connections or malicious interference with the Windows registry.

The results of the malware scan and behavior analysis displayed in the Alerts tab and ranked according to severity, with a higher score being worse than a lower score.

If you opt in for the integrated analysis powered by Carbon Black, you can also view VMS in the Carbon Black Cloud console for further analysis.

Final Recovery

Before being able to recover the virtual machines to the original protected site, when you have completed the validation and identified good candidates, you have to move the VMs to the **stage** step. Moving to the stage step means powering off and staging the VMs for final recovery back to the protected or to an alternate site. During that process, VLCR will take a snapshot of the VMs and remove the security sensor (only on Windows VMs).

NB   The sensor is not automatically uninstalled in Ubuntu VMs.

You can choose to discard all the changes that were made during the recovery and stage with a base snapshot or start over with the last staged snapshot you used to validate the VMs.

To stage a VM, follow this workflow:

- Select one or more VMs from the VM list and Click
  Power off and stage. See Figure 3-27.

Figure 3-27. *End of validation iteration process*

- You will be presented with the option to badge the
  snapshot. You can select to **Take a new staging
  snapshot** or to **Discard changes in recovery SDDC
  and stage with the protected site base snapshot**. In
  that case, any changes made to the VM in this iteration
  will be lost.

- Click the **Power Off and Stage** button to end the
  process. See Figure 3-28.

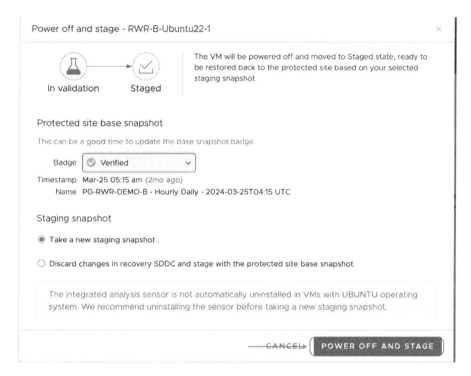

Figure 3-28. *Final step when staging a VM*

Once the VMs have been powered off and staged, they can be recovered to the protected site or to another protected site.

When recovering to the original protected site, the VM itself will replace the original protected VM if it has not been deleted. The original VM will have to be powered off prior to the recovery launch. The objective is to limit the cloud egress impact in cost and transfer time.

During the recovery, the system will check the inventory mappings to make sure that there is no uncertainty on where the VM should be placed. If one mapping is missing, you can remediate it. You can also change the network settings if needed.

If you plan to use an alternate site for the final recovery, you will have to map it as the original site.

If for some reason your protected site is down, you can also recover and run VMs on the Recovery SDDC in VMware Cloud on AWS by leveraging VMware Cloud Gateways on the SDDC.

When you have finished recovering your VM and data, you can end the ransomware recovery process by stopping the Recovery Plan.

The procedure to recover VMs in a protected site is as follow:

- From VM list, select one or more VMs that have been staged.

- From the **Other Actions** menu, click **Recover VMs,**

- Select the original protected site or a different protected site and vCenter to recover VMs.

- Check that each required inventory resource shows a green check mark next to it.

- Confirm the operation (the VM on the protected site will be overwritten). See Figure 3-29.

Figure 3-29. *Recovering a VM on an original protected site*

- Click the **Recover VMs** button to end the process.

- If you have finished recovering the VM, you can now end the recovery process by stopping the plan. See Figure 3-30.

Figure 3-30. *End of ransomware recovery process*

The number of VMs that have been recovered displays with the detail on where they were recovered to. You can click **End Ransomware Recovery** to stop the plan.

NB   You cannot end a recovery plan for ransomware recovery if any VMs are in validation or in the "stage" step.

Remember that when a ransomware recovery plan executes, all snapshot expiration for snapshots taken prior to starting the plan are paused.

After ending a recovery plan, it will revert to a steady state and all retention schedules and retention expiration are going to be resumed according to the defined protection.

3.3 Summary

In this Chapter you have learned more on what ransomware are and how to avoid being infected by them. Like any cyber-attack, a ransomware attack follows a well-established (and smart!) path: Once ransomware enters a system, it begins encrypting individual files or complete file systems to render them and the systems that rely on them unusable.

The America's Cyber Defense Agency published the #StopRansomware Guide that is the one-stop resource to help organizations reduce the risk of ransomware through best practices to detect, prevent, respond, and recover, including step-by-step approaches. Here are some of the key capabilities required to implement the best ransomware recovery solution:

- Secure immutable backup copies. It's also a best practice to have the backup copies operationally air-gapped and immutable to prevent modification.

- **Deep history of backup copies**: Keeping at least three months of data is a best practice when recovering from ransomware as the dwell time can be very long.

- Have a dedicated workflow with guided restore point selection to facilitate the selection of the right point in time copy.

- Rapid iteration of the snapshots to quickly iterate and find the right candidates for restoration.

- Behavioral analysis of the workloads to remove malware during the recovery iteration.

- IRE and isolation of the VM during the recovery process to prevent malware lateral movement in the IRE. It's crucial to not reinfect clean systems during recovery.

VMware Live Cyber Recovery leverages core capabilities and features to provide the ideal last line of defense to recover from ransomware with a set of tools and environment that aligns with the recommendations edited by America's Cyber Defense Agency.

What VMware Live Cyber Recovery offers to customers is the ability to be guided through the recovery process by providing a dedicated workflow.

Conclusion

Addressing the growing threats of ransomware in a more and more
complex IT landscape with both on-premises and cloud deployment
model is getting an overwhelming tasks with multiple challenges. Avoiding
exposing critical data to hackers starts by implementing a set of preventing
measures. But in the unfortunate case of being hit by a ransomware the
only solution is to have a strong recovery plan as this is going to be the
last line of defense. To address and solve the key challenges of recovering
data from a ransomware attack, VMware offers a solution that addresses
both the
on-demand disaster recovery use case as well as the next-gen ransomware
recovery use case.

   When it comes to the ransomware recovery use case, VMware Live
Cyber Recovery provides very powerful capabilities that are truly different
from anything that is out there today, including the following:

- Deep snapshot history spanning hours, days,
  and months

- Recovery from any snapshot without an RTO penalty

- An air-gapped and immutable-by-design system

- Instant power-on

- File/folder restore

- An isolated recovery environment (IRE)

- Restore point validation with embedded behavioral
  analysis

- Push-button VM isolation levels

© Christophe Lombard 2024
C. Lombard, *Mastering VMware Cloud Disaster Recovery and Ransomware Resilience*,
https://doi.org/10.1007/979-8-8688-0829-6

CONCLUSION

A proper ransomware recovery solution requires security, backup, networking, compute, and storage to come together. VMware has uniquely taken all of these elements plus best practices when it comes to recovering from ransomware attacks and put them together into a cohesive and integrated solution that helps customers minimize data loss and accelerate recovery.

Index

Printed in the United States
by Baker & Taylor Publisher Services